D0148511

WITHDRAWN

THE JOHN DEWEY LECTURE

The John Dewey Lecture is delivered annually under the sponsorship of the John Dewey Society. The intention of the series is to provide a setting where able thinkers from various sectors of our intellectual life can direct their most searching though to problems that involve the relation of education to culture. Arrangements for the presentation of the Lecture and its publication by Teachers College Press are under the direction of George Willis, Co-chairperson.

RECENT TITLES IN THE SERIES

Excellence in Public Discourse:
John Stuart Mill, John Dewey, and Social Intelligence
James Gouinlock

Building a Global Civic Culture:
Education for an Interdependent World
Elise Boulding

The Dialectic of Freedom
Maxine Greene

Education for Intelligent Belief or Unbelief
Nel Noddings

Cultural Politics and Education
Michael W. Apple

In Praise of Education
John I. Goodlad

In Praise of Education

John I. Goodlad

Teachers College Press
Teachers College, Columbia University
New York and London

Published by Teachers College Press, 1234 Amsterdam Avenue, New York, NY 10027

Library of Congress Cataloging-in-Publication Data

Goodlad, John I.
    In praise of education / John I. Goodlad.
        p.   cm. — (The John Dewey lecture)
    Includes bibliographical references (p.   ) and index.
        ISBN 0-8077-3621-X (cloth : alk. paper). — ISBN 0-8077-3620-1
(pbk. : alk. paper)
        1. Education—Aims and objectives—United States. 2. Education—
    Social aspects—United States. I. Title. II. Series: John Dewey
    lecture (Columbia University. Teachers College Press)
    LA210.G626   1997
    370'.973—dc21   97-2885

ISBN 0-8077-3620-1 (paper)
ISBN 0-8077-3621-X (cloth)

Printed on acid-free paper

Manufactured in the United States of America

04 03 02 01 00 99 98 97   8 7 6 5 4 3 2 1

Contents

Foreword

John I. Goodlad, in *In Praise of Education*, has once again written a book that will heighten understanding of education and raise the level of public discourse about it. Both accomplishments are far from ordinary, for education is something that everyone experiences continuously yet no one comprehends completely, and something that only a few seem able to talk about in ways that do justice to its essential character.

Education is an ongoing presence in each person's life. Thus, like a living human being, education is something simultaneously concrete yet contradictory, familiar yet ephemeral. In one of its many forms or another, it is something we all are familiar with, something everyone knows well, yet, mysteriously, it is also something only a few know intimately. John I. Goodlad knows it intimately. But not everyone's way of knowing intimately is the same, nor is everyone's way of describing that experience. Hence, this book can be considered a conversation between Goodlad and the reader in which Goodlad describes his experience of knowing education intimately. The book is both a search for wisdom and a love story. Goodlad takes us inside his mind and his heart. The conversation is about the universal truths of philosophers and the existential truths of each of us. It is a fundamentally educative conversation in which we are reminded that education can be defined, but, inevitably, it must also be lived.

In describing education as dealing with both the universal and the particular, Goodlad reminds us that the personal development of individuals always takes place within a social context and, as John Dewey suggested, the word that best describes the most fully educative context is "democracy." Therefore, education and democracy exist in a symbiotic relationship. There is always tension between education for individual autonomy and education for responsible citizenship, but, in the last analysis, what is good for one is good for the other. Describing this idea and quoting Arthur G. Wirth on the Deweyan tradition, Goodlad explains at the beginning of Chapter 2 that his thesis

> is that the proper context for education is a politically and socially democratic one. Not a half-formed democracy of slogans and rituals but a work in progress that continuously explores "how more people can live with a sense of empowered participation." The core idea, exceedingly complex but deceptively simple in appearance, is that democracy in progress must be continuously self-conscious about the degree to which it is safe for education in its fostering of decency, civility, justice, freedom, and caring.

As Dewey pointed out many times, such a democratic society provides conditions conducive to the personal development of intelligent, aware, and active individuals, but, as empowered citizens participating within society, such individuals help create a democracy even more conducive to still more and better individual and democratic social development. And on and on.

The education Goodlad praises is central to this process. His book continues this ongoing Deweyan tradition.

George Willis
for The John Dewey Society Lectures Commission

Preface

Writing a small book, like preparing a small speech, is deceptive in its demands. Conditions of my accepting the invitation to deliver the 1994 John Dewey Lecture provided a head start on the book manuscript to follow that is one of the requirements. At the time, I was beginning to think about a chapter, "Democracy, Education, and Community," I had agreed to write for a book being edited by Roger Soder, *Democracy, Education, and the Schools*, to be published by Jossey-Bass. The tentative outline suggested additional avenues expansion of the chapter into a book would require. I very much appreciate approval of my plan by the three entities involved: Jossey-Bass Publishers and Teachers College Press for agreeing that the chapter in a book published by the former might well appear later in my book to be published by the latter, and the John Dewey Society for accepting this arrangement.

An invitation to spend a month of residency at the Hoover Institution as a Distinguished Visiting (Hanna) Scholar in Educational Policy added an auspicious note. (I am grateful to Lewis B. Stuart and the Four Square Foundation for making this possible.) I would prepare the lecture in January 1994 and deliver it in April at the annual conference of the American Educational Research Association and again in the fall at Teachers College, Columbia University, as agreed. This schedule would give me quite a leg up on the book manuscript due in 1996.

Things do not always work out as planned. Since the John Dewey Society anticipates that the two lecture presentations might well turn out to be two chapters of the book to be written, I envisioned the completion of at least three chapters by fall: the chapter for *Democracy, Education, and the Schools* and two others from the two presentations. Completion of the book manuscript in 1995 now took on the appearance of a reasonable expectation. But the three somehow got wrapped up into a whole that was neither a chapter nor a book. Readers of my chapter in Roger Soder's book will discover only some short segments that reappear in what follows. This paucity of replication led to the realization that delivering a manuscript in 1996, the year initially targeted, was a challenge.

As I settled down to begin anew, the chunks of material already written were as much a hindrance as an asset. The interconnections among the ideas I wished to put forward are such as to create a difficult task of integration without undue repetition. And yet, a degree of repetition appeared both unavoidable and desirable. I set out to spiral a clutch of concepts so that each would emerge more than once to be both revisited and elaborated. In proceeding, I became more and more convinced of the need for this spiraling, both because the concepts are familiar and because they are so commonly ignored. The necessity of pounding them home one more time became compelling. The major concepts are embedded together as often as possible in the narrative, often implicitly, and then singled out for individual treatment.

One of these concepts is of education as exclusively an individual, personal experience—development of a self. One can assist but not "do" education for another. A second concept is of context: There is no self devoid of a culture. A third concept follows: Since one is educated by the entire surround, education is environmentally ubiquitous. A fourth concept addresses the shaping characteristics of this surround: The ideal espoused by the people of the United States of America and many other countries is a work in progress referred to as democracy. In what follows, I concentrate more on social than political democracy—on caring for one another and creating civil communities. Education and democracy share a mutual instrumentality: A flourishing democracy nurtures education; education nourishes democratic character.

This education-democracy symbiosis gives rise to a fifth concept: Education is an inalienable right. It is immoral to deny full development of the self through the denial of access to education. The ubiquitous nature of education necessitates implementation of a sixth concept: There must be continuous, deliberate attention to all of the contextual contingencies to ensure cultivation of individual and collective democratic character. Hence, schools are not sufficient; the entire community must be educative. However, our culture has decreed a vital role for schools as a rite of passage from the narcissism of early childhood to the self-transcendence required for responsible citizenship. A seventh concept emerges: Schools must serve a common public purpose that, above all private purposes, justifies their support as part of our democratic infrastructure.

The eighth concept turns our attention once more to what education is: National ends must not dictate the educational journey of self-transcendence. Such ends are fleeting, almost invariably the result of narrow partisan interests masquerading as the common good. They lay claim to knowledge of a future that justifies and authorizes the educational shaping of the citizenry toward this future. This is mischievous and immoral. The ends a society chooses to state for education must be true to what education is and, therefore, must be both stable and comprehensive, leaving open the possibilities for creating and choosing myriad paths. Only in this way can a society ensure the development of maximum selfhood and the diversity of "selfs" an unknown future will require.

Most of the rest of what follows addresses conditions necessary to the advancement of these interrelated concepts. Among these conditions is one of such significance that it becomes virtually a major concept in its own right. It has to do with an educational curriculum to be advanced by all of our educative agencies and services: a curriculum for development of an ecocentric environmental ethic. Increasingly, this ethic emerges in significance as an essential component of democratic character. In its absence, we will perish. Much more than a small book is required to place and advance it as the agenda for education in a democracy.

My travails in getting this manuscript to press were considerably eased by two people. Once again, Paula McMannon brought to readability the kinaesthetics of head, eye, hand coordination I achieve on my P.E.N. and P.A.D. word processor. Her editorial touch is light, subtle, and significant. The manuscript benefited in several ways from the editorial attention of Timothy McMannon, as well, and particularly from his compilation of the meanings and instrumentalities we have attached to education historically, and his excellent monograph, *Morality, Efficiency, and Reform: An Interpretation of the History of American Education* (Work in Progress Series, No. 5, Institute for Educational Inquiry, Seattle, Washington, 1995). I thank them both.

The pages that follow represent my present perspective on the conceptual grounding of a comprehensive educational improvement initiative conducted through the National Network for Educational Renewal (NNER) described in Chapter 5. The mission and the agenda of the NNER are devoted to the nature and role of education in a democracy: the cultivation of individual and collective democratic character. The Center for Educational Renewal at the University of Washington and the independent Institute for Educational Inquiry in Seattle provide support to this initiative. The total staff of these two agencies, scattered across the United States, comes together periodically for meetings that include both business matters and sustained conversations regarding the conceptual grounding of the whole.

I thank the members of this outstanding group of people for the degree to which they have influenced much of what follows. One of them, Calvin Frazier, brings to these discussions years of experience as a former state commissioner of education and keen awareness of the educational preoccupations of policymakers. The questions he raises have caused me, again and again, to rethink ideas that I had tucked away in my mind as settled, sometimes strengthening and sometimes softening them. One of his most penetrating questions significantly influenced the writing of Chapter 5 in particular. Thanks to Cal and the rest of my colleagues for making my task even more challenging than anticipated and, I trust, improving the outcome.

I have made no deliberate effort in this addition to the John Dewey Lecture Series to delve into Dewey's voluminous writings for passages relevant to my own. Nor have I made any effort to establish independence from his ideas. That would be impossible.

John I. Goodlad
July 1996

In Praise of Education

CHAPTER 1

What Education Is

Education is one of our most ubiquitous phenomena. It pervades the context of virtually the whole of daily living. It constitutes the core of every domain of organized human thought. Education provides the most fundamental canons of human conversation. Donald Vandenberg begins his book on education with a sweeping summary of its ubiquitous character:

> Historically, education is the transmission of the human heritage in order to maintain and enhance the level of civilization a given society has attained. Anthropologically, education is the humanization of the young that occurs in the dialogue between the generations and that enables the young to attain adulthood and a place in adult society. Sociologically, education is the socialization of the young into the societal roles and values believed necessary and desirable for a society's continued existence. Politically, education is the preparation for citizenship in the state or nation. Economically, education is the acquisition of the knowledge, skills, and values necessary for gainful employment and for training the workforce. Existentially, education is becoming aware of the possibilities of being that enable one to achieve an adult presence to the world as a morally and socially responsible person with one's own value and dignity. Cosmically, education is the journey of becoming at home in the universe.[1]

Most statements of the aims of education embrace all of these perspectives. Almost without conscious choice, I address all of them on succeeding pages—testifying one more time to the pervasiveness of education. However, two themes and the tension between them tend to dominate what follows: the process of achieving one's own autonomy and that of simultaneously becoming a responsible citizen. Balanced blending of the two is the path to becoming at home in the universe.

1

Education and Power

Shaping Individual Behavior

Throughout my lifetime, I have heard three voices regarding the shaping of individual behavior: Educate them, pray for them, punish them. The first is a voice of belief in the ability of humans to make judicious use of opportunities to develop and exercise wisdom. It is the voice of education, of reason and hope. Education is temporal; it is a kind of insurance that life will be better here on earth. It is grounded in the terrestrial rather than the heavenly and in finite time rather than eternity. Education connects to the spiritual to the degree that the mind is viewed as God-given.

The second voice is that of faith—faith in the power of divine guidance to lead the lost out of the secular wilderness to salvation of the individual human soul. In contrast to education, religion provides faith when dependence on reason fails. The downed pilot in enemy territory uses everything he has learned to survive—and prays. While I was trying to help incarcerated juvenile delinquents acquire reasoning abilities that might keep them out of mischief, my mother prayed for them.

The voice of punishment is one of fear, despair, futility, or all three. It eschews rational hope and spiritual faith, usually out of fear. Ironically, it is a voice that is most powerful and diabolical when it appears to be couched in educational and religious idioms—when it replaces reason with writs and faith with dogma. The pursuit of both selfhood and salvation are denied. Such is the art of the demagogue.

The theme most central to the drama of history is the struggle of human beings for choice in their development of temporal wisdom and spiritual belief, whether the medium be novel, poem, play, painting, or song. It is a theme that transcends all the rich variations in humankind: a struggle for freedom of thought and expression, of access to knowledge, of belief, and to pray. Expressions of the theme often have been most poignant at moments in history when men and women have been "on the verge," as Maxine Greene puts it: "Confronting a void, confronting nothingness, we may be able to empower the young to create and recreate a common world—and, in cherishing it, in renewing it, to discover what it signifies to be free."[2]

Education and religion have been handmaidens in the drama. Often, they have been at odds, most frequently when the differences between the two are not recognized, when they have been called upon to play similar rather than different roles. They serve the common good best when they are joined symbiotically, each in its own rather than the other's idiom. Excessive preoccupation with the educational or the religious idiom, to the point of making one from the two, leads to mischief. Education has to do with human understandings and power, religion with what lies just beyond. The theologian (and former president of Harvard University) Nathan Pusey suggested that God cannot be fully encompassed by our minds—if you understand something, it probably is not religion.[3] Nonetheless, there is much to learn about religion and spiritual power. Study of the human drama is incomplete without such learning.

Shaping Group Behavior

The power in the ubiquitousness of education is recognized by despots. They seek control of educational media at the outset: publishing, radio and television broadcasting, schools. Meetings, other than official ones, are banned. In Ray Bradbury's *Fahrenheit 451*,[4] the authorities viewed censorship of what went into books as insufficient; they banned and burned them, severely punishing those who possessed them. The educational advisers from the U.S.S.R. to the People's Republic of China put their own biased books about the United States of America on the shelves of the universities, writing them in English to create an appearance of authenticity. These then become a medium of learning English in Chinese secondary schools. In each of the several dozen schools of the People's Republic my colleagues and I visited several years ago, we heard repeated by each of our host principals the same incantations of beliefs to be inculcated in the pupils. They had nothing to do with the aims of education one derives from Vandenberg's comprehensive set of educational perspectives. They had much to do with control of schools in the interest of the state.

Over time in totalitarian societies, the voices of fear and distrust replace those of hope and faith. It is no accident that the use of punishment mimics to the degree possible the most ubiquitous characteristics of education. Conversation is encouraged in order to learn *about* not *from* the views of another. The reward is not in learning from one's fellows but in telling on them to the authorities. Fear grows; freedom dwindles.

When the voice of "punish them" becomes the most ubiquitous in society, shutting off large numbers of people in physical and in-

tellectual prisons, that society becomes like individuals with clogged
arteries and diseased livers. It is in crisis. Fear and intolerance replace education and religion as symbiotic handmaidens; both the
leaders and the citizenry become more and more mean-spirited.
Education is sloganized as an instrument for indoctrination and
training, thus endangering its ability to renew. Religion is ritual-
ized to ease the discomfort of internalizing its precepts as an act of
faith. With official writs proclaimed, it becomes easier to find, label,
and condemn those "of little faith." A nation thus burdened becomes
hostile to freedom, hastening the hardening of its arteries of official truth. And hastening its death. For education is too ubiquitous
not to do its good work over time.

Healthy societies maintain a whole array of educational contingencies that keep them from the verge where discovering what it
means to be free can be submerged by the false premises and promises of the great all-knowing leader. The tasks of keeping in balance
and harmony the voices of reason and hope and of faith while simultaneously calming the voice of punishment in the community are so
daunting that utopias have periodic appeal even in healthy communities. The ideas of John Dewey regarding the making of a democracy,[5] of Jürgen Habermas regarding critical inquiry at the center of
human progress,[6] and of Robert Bellah and colleagues regarding the
good society[7] find favor in some academic circles but are too demanding of time and energy and too lacking in promises of early gratification to have wide appeal in times of rapid change and uncertainty.
Indeed, the practical requirements of implementation appear daunting to many people under the best of circumstances. But utopias come
on ready-made, scant in the requirements for getting there and, consequently, modest in their conceptual and logistical demands. The
contingencies already are there; one simply responds to them. One
does not have to create them. With choices already made in one's best
interests, moral dilemmas are removed or softened. Furthermore, the
contingencies that apply to nonconforming are simply more of the
same. The voice of punishment is thus muted. Utopias are complete
in their appeal.[8] The more comprehensive the vision and the more
detailed the contingencies, the less the need to learn to choose. The
mood inside the utopian compound, presumably, is of paradise
gained. But, from the outside, where the perception more likely is of
imminent combustion, the question is why obvious warning signals
are ignored or not seen.

The lesson that comes through to me in the drama of humankind's struggle for individual liberty in a free society pertains to the

centrality of the mind.[9] Whether authority be derived from cruel tyrant or seemingly benign guru, power lies in numbing the individual mind in favor of groupthink. The full development of selfhood is sacrificed to an imposed common good that smoothes out deviations. We cringe over the brutalities routinely administered to deviants in a tyrannical régime. We are appalled over the lives lost when still another fanatical cult self-destructs. But we are incredibly complacent about—indeed, often serenely untouched by—the millions of selfhoods left adrift in contexts that deny or thwart their fulfillment. Education is so ubiquitous that we fail to comprehend its power and see the consequences of its denial, misuse, and abuse until we are on the verge and in crisis.

Since the crisis lies within the community and is bloodless, with no invaders storming the walls, how do we know we are experiencing one? Where stand the nations of the world today with respect to such a crisis and awareness of it? Where stands the United States of America? Did the National Commission on Excellence in Education that produced that educational call to arms, *A Nation at Risk*,[10] believe that the citizenry could be aroused only by military language invoking images of global economic warfare? Or were its members simply unaware of the growing internal crisis of much more serious nature than the proclaimed poor academic test performance of the nation's children? I would like to believe the former supposition because I so fear the reality of the latter.

Tensions and Dilemmas

At least three critical tensions regarding individual freedom and the making of civil communities come through in the foregoing. First, the pursuit of individual freedom unhinged from all else is self-defeating. Second, the creation of *civitas* (a body of people constituting a politically organized community) requires a level of *civicism* (civic consciousness) that places limits on the exercise of individuality.* Third, the dual demands of self-realization and responsible citizenship are wearying to the degree that more than a few people seek relief through committing responsibility and authority to others. The nature of this exchange is of major import.

---

*I use these words throughout what follows (especially in Chapter 2) without further definition beyond elaboration in context.

These three interrelated tensions are the inheritance of people everywhere.

Self-defeating freedoms are those "the equal exercise of which by all members of society frustrates the very purpose of the freedoms themselves."[11] In seeking to protect against such loss of freedom through its excessive pursuit, communities must create infrastructures that curb such pursuit sensitively. Different kinds of costs inevitably are involved. Many people find themselves paying taxes for services they do not use—roads, parks, baseball stadiums, schools—and protection from hazards that may appear to them to be remote or irrelevant—the enforcement of codes and restrictions regarding their freedom to use the services for which they are taxed. Nowhere are the political battles over the desired infrastructure more marked than in "idyllic" retreats where some people seek to keep the environment pristine and others ("newcomers") want to bring with them the infrastructure left behind (while keeping things pristine). The sharpest controversies pertain to the sanctity of individual property rights over restrictions imposed "for the common good"—a struggle that has spilled a good deal of blood from the early colonial days to the present.

Human beings have resorted to virtually every conceivable array of ways to deal with the individual–group tension. They have been reasonably content for a time during periods of benign despotism, sullen and restless under conquering tyrants, participatory and hopeful in communes, programmed to faith in sectarian ghettos, listless during long periods of bureaucratic specification and control. The shifts from despotism to anarchy and anarchy to despotism often have been rapid—so rapid that there has been little time to profit from earlier learnings. Nonetheless, in many nations throughout the world, a code of civil laws has emerged to retain or restore a reasonably orderly infrastructure.

Tensions of Democracy

Increasingly, nations have looked to democracy as the most promising political answer to the tensions created by the interweaving of individual freedom and community well-being. Democracy is a demanding endeavor and certainly no panacea. But, so far, it appears to be the best arrangement of governance we know and have tried. But no form of government has worked or will work without a social fabric that also is best described as democratic.

Creating and maintaining a community, be it a small village or a huge nation, that nicely balances over time the power that goes with individual freedom and the restraint that goes with *civitas* is always demanding and sometimes precarious. The prospects for balance are dim when development of the minds of the people is curtailed through the denial or corruption of education. Denial to even a few creates a blemish that can grow into cancer and rot. Yet there has not been in the whole of human history a time in the life of any nation unmarked by such blemish. In Western civilization, we refer so admiringly to ancient Greece as to imply an exception. Of course, it was not.

Given this history, then, the rhetoric of expectations for a social and political democracy that would effect this balance first caught and then retained worldwide attention. A fledgling republic, the United States of America, boldly put forward a bill of rights and a constitution designed to guide, advance, and protect a social and political infrastructure that would balance individual freedom and the commonweal. At a time when some men and women were not free citizens, the language appeared to embrace all encompassed within the nation's boundaries—north and south, east and west, from sea to shining sea. A bloody civil war was later fought in large part over the meaning of "all."

Although subsequent rhetoric placed education at the heart of the great American experiment in democracy, reference to its conduct was omitted from the Constitution. The Founding Fathers were prescient in regard to many matters. Were they so prescient as to perceive the ubiquitous working of education in all the villages, towns, cities, and states of the Republic, too ubiquitous for any one segment of government to be the responsible agency? Did they see that democracy and education go hand in hand, that they are inextricably interwoven?

If so, viewing the state of the nation today, they probably would be quite alarmed. While education is widely touted as the road to a robust democracy, financial expenditures to restrain and deny the right to exercise judgment approach the level of expenditures designed to educate people to make wise judgments. The voice of punishment is pervasive and frequently shrill, often drowning out the voice of reason and hope. The voice of faith is increasingly a dissonant cacophony that ignores the importance of the essential differences between education and religion in a productive symbiosis. The three voices are seriously out of balance and, consequently, the nation is in crisis. The crisis runs deep, since so few of our elected leaders appear to sense or heed it.

Dilemmas for Schools

Our schools, we have been told throughout the years, are the bulwark of our democracy. They serve the public purpose of educating our children for the responsibilities of citizenship.[12] But, for some years, we have been told also that our schools no longer are "the foundation of our freedom, the guarantee of our future, the cause of our prosperity and power, the bastion of our security, the bright and shining beacon . . . the source of our enlightenment."[13] They have failed us. They have so failed us, say some critics, that the time is come to separate them "from government-approved schoolteachers who use government-approved textbooks,"[14] to abolish compulsory attendance laws, to separate school and state.

Have the schools failed us or have we failed them? Is it not misguided, politically driven reform that has failed, largely because it directed schools to do what they cannot do, such as create better jobs? And, in trying to do what they cannot do, have schools lost their way, pushed this way and that by changing expectations? Have they lost their way because we, as a people, have forgotten what education is in making schools instrumental to our private, individual ends? Will schools separated from state interest and in the hands of families serve the public interest better? If they do not, how will we ensure the future of our democracy through education?

Or is the perceived connection a romantic Camelot-like illusion that requires instead a dramatic shift from our near-spiritual belief in the improvability of human existence through education to a market-oriented conception that may be more closely geared to the nature of humankind? How would such a shift affect our understanding of what education is and schools are for? Would we need schools or would the rearing of the young in families and the marketplace suffice? Then, brought to the verge, would we desperately seek to restore a more educationally sound version of the schools previously abandoned to the private purpose?

We tend to be impatient with such questions. We find them boring; our minds are made up. But visit them we must. As stated above, the worst crises are within, and persons within are often the last to know. The consequences are grist for historians whose work usually is more predictive of self-fulfilling prophecies than of self-renewing propensities and capacities.

What, Then, Is Education?

There are words for which adjectives are a redundancy. Virtue, truth, beauty, and justice are of this genre. Education is another of these. Strangely, we do not speak of *better* virtue, truth, beauty, or justice, but we do not hesitate to speak of *better* education. This use would not be corrupting with respect to education if it were used only to add emphasis, as Wordsworth might have referred to the *boundless* beauty of his sea of golden daffodils. "Boundless" adds nothing to the concept of beauty but it does not distract either. Modifiers of education draw attention from the meaning of the word.

The adjectives commonly tacked on to education serve primarily organizational and political agendas, distracting us from what education is and what this understanding might purport for an educational agenda. Which word and its attendant concepts is the more likely to dominate in conversations about each of the following: physical education, consumer education, economic education, sex education, career education, environmental education, law education? In conferences on these topics each year, how much of the conversation will address political and organizational strategies and how much the nature of education? The answers to both questions are uncomfortably clear. "Education itself thus becomes both obvious and invisible, a shibboleth and a hollow term."[15]

"Better" is among the more innocuous of the modifiers we use in our talk of education-related matters. Nonetheless, it usually leads us quickly into discussions of resources, restraints, prestige, and how to do "it" better, as though we are agreed on what it is we want done better. By dropping all such modifiers, we are forced to confront just one word, *education*. The difficulty is in sustaining the confrontation. Scarcely into extracting ore from the educational mine in conferences, we welcome the distracting voice: "Let's get off this philosophical kick into the practical. I came here to learn about something new to use next week."

The beauty of words like justice, truth, and education is the way in which peeling off one layer of meaning leads to another and another. The joy is the degree to which one encounters and yet adds to the familiar, like listening to a different orchestra's rendition of *The Four Seasons*. The many definitions of education that have stood the test of time to be often quoted have much in common; yet, there are nuances that stir imagination.

I sometimes ponder why the statement "Education is everywhere the same" by Robert Maynard Hutchins stirred so much controversy among philosophers. The reason becomes apparent in the definitions. They almost invariably contain two major components. The first emphasizes the self and the unique individuality of the educative process: the acquisition of the wisdom that defines self-hood. This, presumably, is at least one part of what convinced Hutchins that education is everywhere the same. This is the component that makes up half of Lawrence Cremin's definition in his reference to the development of sensibilities[16] and nearly all of Israel Scheffler's in his stress on the formation of habits of judgment and the development of character.[17] Indeed, it is the triumph of the self over all else that so often distorts and corrupts the conduct of education, particularly in schools, and subverts the *unum* in *e pluribus unum*. It is imperative, therefore, that conversation about the nature of education become habitual so that the full scope of its meaning will be revealed.

Yet, fixation on the precious, unique individualism of education is understandable. It is so much the essence of freedom that intrusions into its conduct often are passionately resisted. But preoccupation with only the individual component can make of education a self-defeating freedom, the exercise of which leads relentlessly to its loss. *A self cannot be fully realized apart from culture.* "Self-respect presupposes education as initiation into some culture."[18] The exercise of choice regarding those elements of culture to be included in and excluded from the educational process is a risk-laden freedom. Free and open education for all is the best guarantee that this will be a choice wisely made.

A definition of education necessarily includes, then, the development of civility in an individual perceived always as a citizen. Gary Fenstermacher emphasizes this enculturation in his definition, in which human beings "continually enlarge their knowledge, understanding, authenticity, virtue, and sense of place in the past, present and future of the human race."[19]

The wisdom central to self matures in a cultural context through an interplay that is characterized by myriad choices determined by preferences and honed by education for living this sort of life over that. It is this interplay that gives rise to and shapes the educator's role. Choices involve placing one set of beliefs or preferences over another. The choices are moral, reflecting a present state of wisdom. Wisdom, then, is a moral term, as John Dewey effectively argued.[20] Education—the cultivation of wisdom in the cultural context—is a moral undertaking. It follows that teaching the young in schools, in homes, and in the marketplace, and educating teachers for so doing are moral enterprises.

Education Is a Moral Endeavor

The word *moral* carries with it a great deal of varied connotational baggage. When my colleagues and I linked it to teaching as an ever-present dimension,[21] we were simultaneously cheered and challenged. Cheered because, presumably, we were recommending a pedagogical stance in regard to the evils of alcohol, drugs, and extramarital or premarital sex. We were challenged with the query, "Whose moral values shall prevail?" Both the cheers and the challenges missed our intended meaning.

We were reaffirming a position taken by many others: Selfhood is shaped in a context. It matures, for better or for worse, through choosing (or being forced to choose) among alternatives. These alternatives are value-laden; one identifies with some and rejects others. The choices are moral ones.

This observation takes me back to a pivotal question near the end of the preceding section: Might people be served better by enculturation into a market-driven context rather than the more comprehensively altruistic ones so often embraced by definitions of education such as Fenstermacher's? My answer is an emphatic "no"—not just because of moral preference but because such would not suffice the restless curiosity and wondering that drives human beings (to which Scheffler refers in the balance of his definition of education). An economic model for education is insufficient, simply because it fails to embrace the whole of what it means to be human. There are those several other perspectives put forward in the initial quotation from Vandenberg at the beginning of this chapter.

Regardless of the dissonance stirred by referring to education as a moral endeavor, not to address the word *moral* leaves us with "a shibboleth and a hollow term," as Donna Kerr sees "education" to be when only modifiers are the subject of conversation. This is what happens to education when we use *moral* as an adjectival modifier as in *moral education*. All education is moral. Placing the word *moral* in front of *education* is not a redundancy that adds emphasis. It misleads, taking us into the cheers, challenges, and controversies referred to earlier.

So long as we are clear on the two-dimensional nature of education—the individual and the context, never one without the other—

we can move productively to our aspirations for both individual and context. John White suggests that we put aside the issue of whose morality should prevail and seek development in the individual of those dispositions that pertain to others' well-being. This forces him into a position regarding context: in his view, a democratic one that promotes equality, fairness, freedom, and justice.[22]

There is no way to sanitize education, to erase from it all moral trappings. To suggest, for example, that we pass along to the young the knowledge they need free of moral accouterments is to suggest what cannot be. Often, what is intended in such suggestions is that these, rather than those, moral positions are acceptable. It is difficult to envision even training divorced from moral context. Education is unavoidably a moral endeavor; to view it otherwise is to have in mind something else. The implications for the function and conduct of schooling are enormous.

Education is, in part, everywhere the same in that it always involves interplay between individual and context. But there the sameness ends. In its conduct and consequences, it differs from person to person and place to place according to what is denied and offered access to and what is dominant in the belief systems of the context. The way in which this context shapes selfhood depends heavily on the past and present hierarchy of dominance among the voices of reason and hope, faith, and punishment. Where reason and hope and faith reign supreme, one finds renewing individuals in a renewing society.

The Educative Interplay

I began this essay with the observation that education is ubiquitous. The whole of the interplay between individual and context is educative. Lawrence Cremin has observed that it is folly to talk about educational improvement and excellence apart from the educational influence of families, peer groups, television and radio broadcasting, the workplace, and more.[23] Individuals are so shaped by all of these that it is exceedingly difficult, if not impossible, to sort out their respective contributions. Today, when there are so many powerfully educative forces at work, attributing societal malaise or triumph to any one is irresponsible guesswork. Nonetheless, it is fashionable to target the public schools in particular for malaise.

The conventional focal point for affixing blame or credit to an educational program or initiative is outcome. The linear rationality involved fits nicely with longstanding (but outmoded) input-output industrial models of productivity. But the paradigm is wrong and misleading. The number of contributors to *educational* outcomes are too many and the relationships among them too complex to permit the reliable determination of selective attribution. Even rough approximations require time, money, and effort we rarely are willing to commit and are not cost effective in regard to the insights gained.

Because of this complexity, we opt for something much easier, such as short-answer tests assumed to be valid surrogates for the complex sensibilities and sensitivities implied in our lofty aims for education and schooling. In seeking to improve such measures, we increasingly select surrogates that lend themselves well to quantification but relate poorly to our educational expectations. When these procedures ultimately come to drive educational processes, the educative interplay becomes a mechanistic exercise in training. Managers then mistake these measures and the exercises they come to promote for education. Maintaining the system soon overshadows attention to the educative propensities sought and the critical differences between the two.[24]

Ironically, reform eras, whatever their initial moral intentions,[25] soon fixate on outcomes (outputs) and ways to improve them (inputs). Pose tougher grade-passing standards for students, promise merit pay for teachers who produce higher performance, and out of the black box of school and classroom will come greater outcomes. What goes on in them is ignored. The turbulence created by these external gyrations, embellished by patriotic rhetoric regarding the nation's future, goes unstudied with no derivation of lessons for the next round of school reform. But, inside the boxes, the perturbations must be reckoned with—absorbed, put aside, countered, or whatever. Time and energy that might have been used by students and teachers to inquire into and improve the educative process are squandered. The predictable failure of school reform strikes again.[26] Students and teachers get the blame but the reformers never seem to get the message.

It is the interplay and the players in educative encounters that warrant and beg our attention and support. What attributes characterize the context? What orientations do the individuals involved bring to this context? What norms govern the interactions? In schooling, these questions of educational value come down to such matters as the authenticity of subject matter, readiness of the students, the concept of authority prevailing in the learning and teaching, and so on. Inquiry into these matters leads to hypotheses about educational qualities and to revisions in subject matter, the pacing of students, and the modes of connecting the two. Conditions of educational renewal are activated.

Toward Environments Hospitable to Education

The voice of education usually is synchronized to individual human aspirations (freedom, for example) devoid of context. We state and restate lofty aims for individuals but leave out the circumstances necessary to their fulfillment. Presumably, in its power and majesty, education will bring human beings triumphantly through earthly vicissitudes. And, with God's help, says the voice of religion, the passage beyond will be smoothed. Nations create formal systems of education to manage the delivery of educational programs to the people. As argued above, criteria of efficiency, particularly of cost effectiveness, rank high. It is fascinating to note the degree to which delivery mechanisms divert and consume resources intended to enrich educative processes.[27]

The Schooling (Business) Syndrome

The expansion of schooling in the second half of the 19th century accelerated a search for efficient models of management. There arose a system devoted to regulating the entry, passage, and exit of students grouped by age and grade. To this, students and parents adjusted as one does to a given such as the basic requirements of driving an automobile. There are refinements over the years such as electronically operated steering and signaling mechanisms. Nonetheless, one's attention is directed to what the automobile requires (what the school requires for the successful passage of the student through it). Auxiliary enterprises of instruction and even research grow up around the questions of what automobiles and schools require. Individuals become the units of selection in a psychology of adjustment and adaptation.

Over time, the central features (regularities, Seymour Sarason calls them)[28] of the driving machine become highly valued in their own right. Indeed, they take on a patina that grows lovelier in the eyes of their caretakers with each successive year of polishing these antiques. Even teachers, who should be sensitive to the demands these regularities place upon them, come to echo their meanings and accompanying language. There is conversation about children not ready for school, who cannot learn, who detract from others' learning, who should not be promoted to the next grade or allowed to graduate. A complex system and field of management, supervision, and monitoring and a corps of engineers and researchers attend to maintaining and refining the machinery. Linda McNeil writes poignantly of the dissonance between the contingencies of the system and the interpretation by sensitive teachers of what the setting requires to be educative.[29]

With millions of young people to be processed through the system and so many entering each year, it is easy to understand why and how an auxiliary system grew up around the demands of helping them cope, on one hand, and of keeping the system functioning, on the other. These emphases become sharply evident in analyses of faculties of schools and colleges of education in universities. Commonly, well over half of the education faculty members in any given institution are in the subfields of psychology and administration. The third large group, professors of curriculum and instruction, also devote most of their attention to things that fit into or advance the system. A faculty of 60 or so members commonly has only one philosopher and one historian. It probably has no anthropologist or political scientist, perhaps one part-time economist, and perhaps a cadre of two or three sociologists. Those specialists and generalists most likely to study and raise questions about the system and its functioning are missing or in short supply. Perhaps this explains the conspicuous absence of professors of education in the widespread calls for systemic school reform that erupted in 1983 and 1984[30] and their very modest degree of involvement since. The "academic" attack on the public system of schooling has come primarily from individuals, especially economists, in various independent think tanks and policy centers.

These critics are often on target in regard to systemic excesses and shortcomings. But they almost invariably bring to bear only the canons of assessment derived from their own fields. They rarely bring also that intimate knowledge of the territory that leads to sound hypotheses of remediation. Having caught the attention of policymakers by critical analyses of bureaucracies grown bloated, for example, they now enjoy a reputation of expertise they do not possess and are called upon to come up with blueprints for something to replace what is to be demolished. The Peter Principle is invoked one more time: The able critic is expected to exercise expertise beyond his or her level of competence.[31] The results usually disappoint.

Those who would sweep away the existing system tend to speak both vaguely and glowingly of the educational meccas that will result. But the scope of their intentions is virtually filled with what is to be obliterated and replaced by presumably simpler organizational arrangements. We are not to be bothered with educational details even though the devil resides in the details. The success stories of individual schools that appear to be places of learning and joy, schools that have blossomed within or in spite of the system, commonly are waved aside as the rare product of able, charismatic leaders. Would-be reformers within the system are inspired by stories such as that of Jill Andrews regarding the creation and maintenance for decades of a school environment hospitable to education.[32] But critics of the system would view it as evidence of consuming too much time and energy in the lives of a succession of principals, teachers, superintendents, and others who made it all happen. This observation is not one to be quickly dismissed.

Yet, the heady notions of bureaucracies cast aside so that creativity now restrained will be unleashed to bring forth thousands of exciting schools have about them the myopic unreality of utopias briefly envisioned. Three powerful sets of unavoidable realities are ignored or pushed into the shadows. First, get beyond the lofty aims and purposes of education in schools and one discovers that the foremost function to be fulfilled is a custodial one. Conducting it well is what parents most want and see most ignored by reformers.[33] Second, assuming the system now dismantled, the absence of educational context in our oft-repeated aims and purposes of both education and schooling is revealed. Also revealed is the absence of an agenda around which to rally the eager voyagers now separated, they hope, from the vexing restraints of the schooling syndrome. Third, confronted with a clean slate, persons taking on the tasks of designing the new—be it an elementary, secondary, or tertiary school or some other institution that has had quite a long history—search in their minds for familiar artifacts. The shape and then the details of the new begin to look surprisingly, and often pleasingly, like the old friend they rather enthusiastically believed had been put to rest. The new blueprints are very similar to those for the edifices abandoned.

Healthy Contexts for Education and Schooling

The common omission of context in our aims for education creates the impression that the bringing of educational opportunities (not defined) to individuals will push back whatever evils are storming the walls. Then education will take care of human aspirations within, including the creation of a strong and just community or nation. Education transformed into schooling will eliminate poverty, crime, injustice, and urban blight, and ensure jobs and the nation's security. Nations will become robust because of the excellence of their schools. Consequently, school reform is virtually an ongoing necessity.

This is dangerous thinking that runs counter to history. Healthy nations have healthy schools; schools become healthy as their local and national contexts become healthy. Schools mirror society; they do not drive it. Making schools appear powerfully instrumental, particularly to the individual good, invites their exploitation for private ends. The public purpose of schooling is lost. Education drains from them. Schools cease to serve the common good and, therefore, to be safe havens for education.

A society always should be investing in schools protected from the erosion of their public purpose—that is, the educating of persons committed to a society that nurtures its members. We come to a circuitous path: Virtuous societies sustain education that educates individuals to be virtuous citizens who sustain virtuous societies that . . . This condition is not simply reciprocity: The grateful citizen gives back to a nurturing society. It is, rather, the ubiquitous meshing of self and context that simultaneously shapes wisdom, altruism, and community and gives rise to descriptive words such as virtue, the word Pericles saw as best describing what was valued in his Athenian democracy.[34]

In focusing intensely on school reform for an unprecedented period of time, we have kept obscured the question of whether our schools are now safe for this education. We confound their purpose with expectations for social engineering (create better jobs) and religious exhortation (provide time for prayer). We propose to divorce them from the federal government that forcefully pushed the civil rights interest of equal access for all of our people when some states and localities were blind to it. Either we have forgotten the public purpose of schooling or we have an incredibly benign view of the degree to which we already have a virtuous social democracy. If the latter be so, how did we come to this ideal polity that attends to the good of all? Surely because of our schools, if we give credence to the rhetoric of most of this century.

Then why is it imperative that we now dismantle our system of schooling? Because the context of daily life is so educative that schools devoted to public purpose are no longer necessary? Because we all will acquire wisdom and virtue in the streets and marketplaces through *paideia*? I think not. Rather, I believe that the sudden shift from politically driven reform to make our schools better to politically driven exhortation to privatize schools of choice is evidence that even the political democracy we have striven so hard to attain is adrift from its moral moorings. Instead of politicians seeking to make democracy safe for education and education the handmaiden of democracy, we have too many heeding the special interests they believe will keep them in office. Is the considerable current public interest in the use of schools for private purposes of such political significance as to stimulate politicians to scuttle the public purpose of schooling? Or are schools serving the public purpose viewed as so formidable an obstacle to the unbridled exercise of power that political leaders seek subtle ways to downsize this role? Either way or with the two perspectives in tandem, both social and political democracy lose.

Readers may regard the above paragraph as too harsh an indictment of the current state of both our democracy and our political leaders. But when one thinks carefully about the degree to which politicians of all political stripes and offices have used our schools for their own ends and pandered to special interests with the schools as both bait and barter, the sentences begin to appear to be understatements. And then, when one adds media quivering in unison over outrageous claims regarding the schools as the cause of every ill in the corpus of our society, a rage rises within. How does one explain away the outcry over the schools when polls of a few years ago ranked Japan as the world's economic leader for years to come and the dead silence a few years later when the same polls ranked the United States as first at that time and into the future? Benjamin Barber is right on target when he writes "society undoes each workday what the school tries to do each school day."[35]

We know enough to have good schools everywhere. The body of literature on how we—children especially—learn is deep and comprehensive. There is a comparably useful body of knowledge about shaping the context to maximize the probability that the self will mature in ways that are respectful of others. There is a growing literature on caring pedagogy that cultivates this mutuality. Further, we are fortunate in having or having had some seminal initiatives in school improvement, several accompanied by research, that provide useful trails for others to follow. These tell us, for example, a good deal about the conditions necessary to change and about approaches that should not be repeated.

Most of this knowledge and insight lies fallow. It lies fallow for at least two closely related reasons. The first is a complex array of circumstances that surround the schooling occupation: the legacies of teaching as a low-status, female occupation; the rise of administration as a higher status career line often separated from teaching and connected to business management; the transfer of prestige deprivation from school teaching to colleges of education and the increasing isolation of colleges of education from both the schools and the rest of the university; the emergence of a university reward system favoring research but not teaching or service or the popularization of research; the accompanying separation of research productivity in education from research dissemination and utilization; the exacerbation of this separation by ways in which the preservice education of teachers was controlled from without and hobbled within the university; the increased use of in-service education as a means of refining approved and desired school district practices; and more.

The second reason the knowledge and insight that could be harnessed to renew our schools goes largely unused is even more complex and difficult to pin down. Its elements include the circumstances surrounding the schooling occupation just listed; the widespread personal experience of the population with schooling that democratizes expertise to the point where nearly everyone claims some; the pervasiveness of the assumption that everyone knows what education is; inflated expectations for schools and manipulation of these expectations in the service of special interests; ambiguity in the meaning of the omission of federal responsibility for education in the Constitution; further ambiguity regarding the private interests of citizens in the public schools they support with tax dollars; varying interpretations of the meaning and legitimacy of compulsory schooling; disagreement regarding implementation of church and state separation doctrine; sensitivity to the risk-laden nature of teaching; and much more.

The risk-laden nature of teaching, especially of the young, tends to be viewed from only the private and not the public perspective, however. It is necessary and understandable that parents be deeply interested in what teachers selected to be responsible for children are teaching them. But this interest should be twofold: in both the self and the transcendence of self to identify with and relate to the rest of humanity. Because an important part of this transcendence has to do with citizenship in one's community and nation, there is a public interest in which the state plays a role. Consequently, the state has an interest in the responsible role to be played by parents who choose to home-school. The educational context must provide simultaneously for dispositions of personal efficacy and for those that attend to the well-being of others. This, presumably, is the basic requirement of education in a social and political democracy.

What Follows

The central focus of this little book is the role of education in balancing the tension between personal autonomy and responsible citizenship. This requires tempering freedom with self-imposed restraints so that the exercise of freedom is not self-defeating. The polity needs to be exceedingly self-conscious regarding the extent to which individuals are exercising this self-discipline, just as it needs to be self-conscious about the degree to which government-imposed restraints protect freedom. There has been growing world-wide agreement that democracy is the most promising political arrangement for maintaining this balance.

What also has become increasingly apparent, however, is that there must be an array of nongovernmental arrangements to sustain the human relationships essential to collective living—to community. Apparent, too, is the need for mutual caring developed to the level of habit, caring that comes to embrace human diversity. And everyone needs to learn the arts of disciplined conversation and inquiry essential to resolving differences and solving problems—conditions of the renewing self and the renewing society. These are the processes and fruits of education.

The American democracy—both political and social—is at a critical stage of development. We have become aware that the natural resources that made this nation economically healthy are not inexhaustible. We are much less aware of the degree to which this resource-based wealth washed over so much else in our infrastructure, in effect sustaining in a near-universal system of schooling intellectual capital to compensate for the loss of social capital in moving from an agrarian to an industrial and then technological economy. Our schools became in our eyes not just the symbol but the cause of our well-being.

The shift from worldwide dependence on natural resources to creativity in multiplying the market value of derivatives and, indeed, in worldwide marketing profoundly changed the character of global economic competition and the health of national and local economies. The United States, caught off guard, blamed her schools. There followed a decade of politically driven school reform, more rhetorical than substantive, that took our attention away from serious problems beyond the schools and obfuscated their educational purposes.

My preoccupation with the larger educative context is not intended to downplay the importance of school renewal. Indeed, I devote an entire chapter and parts of others to some of what I have learned from decades of studying and participating in school improvement and to suggestions for making our schools better. However, I fear that neither the initiatives in which I am involved nor those inspired by the good work of James Comer, Linda Darling-Hammond, Howard Gardner, Henry Levin, Deborah Meier, Theodore Sizer, and others will flourish if we count on schools alone for the education democracy requires. We must get more out of the rest of the educational infrastructure, that cacophony of teaching referred to by Lawrence Cremin, than a jumble of information, titillation, and advertising geared to the satisfaction of individual wants.

This cacophony lacks lyrics and orchestration. Donna Kerr would say that it lacks a soul;[36] Seymour Sarason that it lacks a sense of the sacred.[37] It lacks a sense of the meaning of education, what it means to be educative, and conversation regarding the two. Lacking such, this gaggle of voices and instruments often is as tolerant of mean-spiritedness, violence, and intolerance as it is supportive of virtue. Equating education with schooling relieves the rest of society from educative responsibility.

Unfortunately, this does not make the schools safe havens for education, since the schools are so porous with respect to what comes in from without. The ups and downs of test scores tell us little about the health of education in schools. Many of the schools we appear to want to clone are those that produced executives unable to look first to themselves rather than schools to explain their corporate woes, and political leaders more ready to answer the voices of punishment with more prisons than the voices of hope with a robust system of schooling. We must turn our concerted attention to making democracy safe for education.

We turn next, then, to the relationship between education and democracy and then to the educative community (Chapters 2 and

3). The educative community, in turn, provides the hospitable context for schools to rise above their custodial function in serving both their private and their public purpose (Chapter 4). Chapter 5 addresses the conditions the nourishment of education requires, particularly the teachers and teaching a nurturing society ensures. A short concluding chapter celebrates the role education plays in developing the unique self.

There will be readers who view my concern regarding the present state of our democracy and the climate for education to be overheated. Both are secure, they will say, the issues having only to do with agreeing on the conditions necessary to their further advancement. But I am chilled by incidents such as the disdainful comments of a presidential candidate on the "worship of democracy": "Like all idolatries, democratism substitutes a false god for the real, a love of process for a love of country."[38] And by the comment of one of his fans: "Education is a socialistic entity."[39] We must expect and get more from our political leaders than the rhetorical bashing of democracy and education on the campaign trail.

These are not isolated views. They shake one into the realization that the rhetorical tributes we pay to democracy and education can readily lull us into the belief that all is well. Donna Kerr reminds us gently of the work to be done:

> Maybe for purposes of reminding ourselves of our common hunger and our common need for nourishment, we could develop political and economic unions dedicated expressly to promoting conditions conducive to nurturing ourselves and one another. Maybe such associations could themselves give us a sense of solidarity to press for the abandonment of activities and policies erosive of civic society and for the adoption of corporate and governmental plans to enhance civic society. Possibly we could do these things. . . . No other stakes could be so high.[40]

CHAPTER 2

Education and Democracy

There is a contextual surround that invariably shapes the educational process. The political context is critical. The shaping that takes place in a fascist or communist régime is quite different from that in a democracy. The social context is equally, or perhaps even more, critical. People who live by sword and gun raise their children by very different beliefs than do people who value negotiation as the proper way to resolve disagreements.

In that education shapes the self in cultural context, education is everywhere the same. In the nature of this interaction, education is everywhere different. In the spirit of pluralism, some people defend the attainability and even the existence of good schools quite apart from the characteristics of their context. This is to confuse education and schooling. Schooling can be good in its achievement of official public purpose but not provide good education in a context dominated by repression and punishment.

My thesis, introduced in Chapter 1 and woven throughout succeeding pages, is that the proper context for education is a politically and socially democratic one. Not a half-formed democracy of slogans and rituals but a work in progress that continuously explores "how more people can live with a sense of empowered participation."[1] The core idea, exceedingly complex but deceptively simple in appearance, is that democracy in progress must be continuously self-conscious about the degree to which it is safe for education in its fostering of decency, civility, justice, freedom, and caring. Such fostering is not the responsibility nor within the capability of schools alone.

As stated in Chapter 1, the tension in the provision of education and schooling in a democracy is a reflection of the tension within democracy itself—between the rights and responsibilities of the individual and the polity. Maintaining an appropriate balance strains a democratic government. This balance is a condition to be sought, not the norm. Benjamin Barber has stated the challenge well: "Democracy is anything but a 'natural' form of association. It is an extraordinary and rare contrivance of cultivated imagination."[2]

The shadow hanging over Convention Hall was the question of whether the American people could govern themselves—in the sense of balancing the individual and the commonweal. Education came to be seen as the essential condition to be in place. Yet the Founding Fathers left it out of the Constitution. Were they so prescient as to realize that education is both so pervasive and so powerful that it must always be protected and promoted by government but never used as an instrument of government?

Beyond Political Democracy

Making *political democracy* work is a complex, delicate process. Even more complex and precarious is *social democracy*: the living together of people endeavoring to follow democratic principles. People who run away from the bureaucracies that characterize all genres of democracy and, indeed, government are staggered by the interpersonal difficulties encountered in seeking to establish small communes characterized by the utopian principles they envisioned. They soon come to realize how necessary and difficult it is to expand the few values shared to a much larger common core. When the concept of a social democracy is broadened to include all people in a democracy that embraces humankind and the human condition, the problems of resolving religious, ethnic, and racial differences appear overwhelming. Yet, that spark of hope never dies out. Beyond divisiveness there is that *democracy of the human spirit* that transcends all individuality and binds humankind—somewhere a place for all of us, together.

Political democracy depends heavily on traditions, customs, and laws. Social democracy depends heavily on the exercise of civility and *civitas*.* Citizens are not born with the necessary traits; they are acquired through education. The role of education in developing these traits is not at all free from disputation. But disagreement

---

*Because the contemporary definition of *civitas* denotes a politically organized community, more than civility is required for its sustenance and orderly functioning. There is also a framework of civil law.

heightens to a level of violence when the route to a democracy of the human spirit is the subject at hand. How are the differences within, let alone between, secular and sectarian belief and dogma to be pushed aside sufficiently to permit the emergence of a common center?

Even to suggest common ground where two such differing paths to truth join in a sense of the sacred sufficient to provide a moral grounding for democracy—political, social, and of the human spirit—is to bring down on each a pox from the other. And yet, the future of civilization depends on there being widespread agreement on "the sense of interconnections among the individual, the collectivity, and ultimate purpose and meaning of human existence."[3] No such agreement is possible if there are not in the culture educational contingencies that subject all belief to intense scrutiny. The essence of democracy is freedom to engage in this scrutiny with impunity. This means that the very principles on which democracy rests are not immune from inquiry.

A political democracy requires for its sustenance the reiteration of truths and widespread allegiance to them. The more comprehensive these truths and the more commonly shared, the more sustaining the democracy subscribing to them will be. In this, the American democracy is widely regarded as a model, a haven for the oppressed and dissident seeking amnesty. First, we have the "self-evident" truths and unalienable rights of the Declaration of Independence: "that all men are created equal; that they are endowed by their Creator with certain unalienable rights; that among these are life, liberty, and the pursuit of happiness." Then, we have the Constitution to secure them; then the amendments (the first ten of which are known as the Bill of Rights) that assist interpretation and implementation.[4] And to guide the process of ratification for the years that followed, there is that lasting monument to Alexander Hamilton, James Madison, and John Jay, their incredible analysis of every part of the Constitution, *The Federalist*.[5] To make it all more human, we continue to commemorate the Founding Fathers, particularly John Adams, Benjamin Franklin, Alexander Hamilton, Thomas Jefferson, James Madison, and George Washington. We are blessed, indeed, with a comprehensive picture of the good work to be carried out by the citizens, the elected representatives of these citizens, and their agencies in sustaining the American democracy.

It is appropriate for a government to sustain a system of education to ensure among the citizens both understanding of and belief in this comprehensive picture. Many years before a republic was forged, the householders of the early towns taxed themselves for schools in which all the young would be taught "the laws of the land, and the principles of religion." Since they did not need schools for themselves (they could afford tutors and the luxury of sending their children abroad or, eventually, to private academies at home), this self-taxing would appear to be an act of considerable magnanimity. But it was as much, or more, motivated by self-interest.[6] These comparatively prosperous settlers did not want the religion and the ideals of self-government they had brought with them to be endangered by the ignorance of growing numbers of newcomers lacking access to schooling.

These early schools—and those of many decades to follow—had a comparatively easy time of it with respect to mission. The Christian faith and the laws of community living were seen virtually as one. Home, school, and church worked together in a common sense of what it meant to be human in the image of Jesus Christ, the Son of God, and to have liberty under God. But the siren call of freedom was to attract to this land those of other faiths, no faith, other beliefs, and even other gods. The mix was, in time, to sorely test and strain the great democratic experiment.

The resiliency of democracy was further strained and the role of schools muddied by the inexorable rise of "the human individual in his own idiom,"[7] driven by the intrusion of rationalism into all aspects of political, social, and personal life. "The conduct of affairs, for the Rationalist, is a matter of solving problems, and in this no man can hope to be successful whose reason has become inflexible by surrender to habit or is clouded by the fumes of tradition."[8] The moral theory pervading the pursuit of individuality embraced the relationships among the individual, the self, and others. "But as a rational human being he will recognize in his conduct the universal conditions of autonomous personality; and the chief of these conditions is to use humanity, as well in himself as in others, as an end and never as a means."[9]

There appears to be little resolution between the concept of the human being as the creature of God and the concept of self-realization through a process of independent choice. How are both to be served equitably in a modern system of representative government? And what rights of the citizen and duty to government is that government to protect and promote? The laws that come down from legislative bodies favor individual freedom, including the freedom of religious belief and observance.

Political democracy can never resolve dissonance in the fundamental beliefs of its citizens, nor should it. Nor should these citizens expect such resolution. The best a democratic régime can do in this domain is to recognize freedom and support the conditions that sustain it. The end purpose of this freedom goes beyond unabating celebration of the democratic state. The ideal of freedom and of democracy is the autonomous individual who transcends narcissism in the internalization of oughts and shoulds that lead to moral action in the moral community.[10]

The internalization of oughts and shoulds that lead to moral action in the moral community requires a conception of what society should be. "The vision explicitly rules out individualism as an *exclusive* basis for judging proposals for action. The thrust of the vision is that . . . the bond to be forged will contribute more to societal well-being than either a riveting on individual rights or on a suffocating conformity to a collectivity."[11] The current problem of the American democracy is that of coping with a virtual explosion of individuals and collectives seeking to define their identity for themselves in the face of realization that those in power over the years have been defining it for them. This drive for long-overdue recognition and a secure place in the culture (for minorities, women, gay people, disabled people, religious groups, and the like) has been accompanied also by a narcissistic obsession with self that has both hurt just causes and strained community. With the public interest being constantly redefined to accommodate diversity, the core of common vision shrinks, at least until the commonalities of diversity are built into that common core.

It is appropriate to keep education always in view as the long-term hope for sustaining a common core of beliefs and accommodating diversity simultaneously. But the creation of high value and high visibility for education fuels the desire of diverse interest groups to make it work for them. This makes it very difficult for education to serve the commonweal. The problem is exacerbated when education is equated with schooling, as is largely the case in the United States. Then, with the schools becoming instrumental in the cacophony of private purpose attached to them, it is exceedingly difficult for them to know, let alone serve, the public purpose of education.

For education to undergird the renewal of both political and social democracy, it must transcend the divisions in philosophical and religious persuasion that exist in a diverse population and reach for some higher and more universal meaning of human existence.

That there will be agreement on a common set of values and moral principles is unrealistic, if only because such a notion is secular and eschews the concept of divine law embedded in religious belief. But we do know that the study of religions leads to an understanding of their commonalities and respect for their differences as well as for their most common characteristic—faith. Similarly, we know that the study of humankind leads to an understanding of the principles of civility, personal decency, interindividual and intergroup respect, as well as the caring necessary to community. And we learn of the human misery that accompanies the absence of these. Although we may not be able to come together in a common vision, the opportunity to pursue one's own depends on a significant proportion of the population being sufficiently educated to understand and appreciate what is required for the survival and advancement of civilization. So far, human ingenuity appears not to have created for the cultivation and use of intelligence a better instrumentality than a robust political and social democracy.

Education and Self-Transcendence

The dilemma for education as the hope for sustaining a balance between individuality and civicism is its very nature. Education is of and by the self. It cannot be given or taken away by another or performed for one's self by another. There can be no delegation to surrogates. Yet, education is not a private matter. As I have said, there is always a cultural context. There can be no definition and development of self apart from culture. The broader the context of enculturation, the better the prospects for education and for a self capable of participating comprehensively in the human conversation.

Beyond Training

The narcissism of the young child is exhaustively documented and abundantly clear. The process of self-transcendence from self-preoccupation to self-identification to multiple contextual connections and cultural identification cannot be taken for granted.[12] Unfortunately, there is precious little parental preparation for arranging the necessary educational contingencies, a situation that steadily grows worse in this nation. The nature of these contingencies during the months of infancy and years of early childhood is particularly crucial.[13] This formative stage is very short, often providing a parental internship in childrearing that parents hope will serve them well the next time around.

Erik Erikson provided us with both a disturbing and a challenging portrait of the tensions between positive and negative tendencies in his "eight stages of man" through which he says we pass in the life cycle. He stresses the "ritual practice" in the community—the common faith—that supports the development of trustworthiness, autonomy, initiative, industry, identity, intimacy, generativity, and ego integrity that are the characteristics of wholesome individuality: the indices of healthy self-transcendence. Similarly, he notes the significance of what must be ritually eschewed or even proclaimed evil in the community, such as individual mistrust.[14] Although the educating and the paths pursued are of the self, the shaping of that self in family, school, and community is powerful and relentless. And, clearly, the educative agencies are multiple.

The message is clear: "There will be no liberty, no equality, no social justice without democracy, and there will be no democracy without citizens and the schools that forge civic identity and democratic responsibility."[15] If education were merely some kind of training—such as to paddle a canoe, ride a bicycle, or even add numbers—we could afford to be somewhat relaxed about its context. But even under such circumstances we cannot afford not to address the question of ultimate use. My incarcerated students in the industrial school for (delinquent) boys frequently offered to teach me the craft of lock picking. They offered with it no accompanying manual or lessons regarding the moral circumstances under which use of my new skill would be legitimate.

One begins to understand the motivation among some people for a system of schooling required to be scrupulously devoid of moral teaching or of one required to be scrupulously attentive to the ideological mandates of those in control. Pedagogy designed to develop critical-thinking abilities is ruled out in both instances. In the first, parents can be reasonably comfortable with their expectation that what has been carefully taught at home will not confront alternatives at school. In the second, authoritarian officials can be reasonably comfortable that few of the seeds that grow into questioning and revolt will be planted. In both instances, not only is there no need for a liberally educated teaching force, there is disinterest in such—and certainly no interest in the professional education of teachers, especially that part designed to prepare teachers for the moral stewardship of our schools. The mentoring of new teachers into the well-established, noncontroversial ways of the old suffices;

the salaries of teachers and the costs of teaching are kept low. Citizens with no desire to keep critical enculturation out of the schools, who simply have not thought about the connection between education and democracy, are pleased with taxes kept low.

The 1986 slogan of the National Governors' Association, "better schools mean better jobs"[16]—repeated over and over into the 1990s—sells better politically than "education for democracy." When, in the fall of 1993, one very thoughtful governor—Roy Romer of Colorado—managed to inject Jeffersonian concepts into a meandering discussion of schooling on the program *This Week with David Brinkley*, William Bennett (presumably then an aspirant for a run at the presidency) waved him aside as if Jefferson had engaged in idle dreaming. This from a former secretary of education.

Increasing attempts from a wide array of special interest groups—strange bedfellows who will divide and quarrel bitterly once they succeed in enfeebling the educative function of our public schools and creating a unique model of private schools sustained by the public purse—both wittingly and unwittingly threaten all three of the democracies defined earlier in this chapter. What appears to drive most of these groups is a kind of individualism that shuns self-transcendence and the making of a democratic polity. They are endowed by their Creator with unalienable rights: *my* life, *my* liberty, and *my* pursuit of happiness. The words triggering their attack on the public schools include equity, cooperative learning, global education, heterogeneous grouping, and critical thinking—and any others that speak to social democracy—and any concepts that appear to challenge a given group's aspirations for hegemony. After expressing his alarm, Barber reaffirms the imperative:

> Education in vocationalism, pre-professional training, what were once called the "servile arts" . . . may be private. But public education is general, common, and thus in the original sense "liberal." This means that public education is education for citizenship. . . . The autonomy and the dignity no less than the rights and freedoms of all Americans depend on the survival of democracy: not just democratic government, but a democratic civil society and a democratic civic culture. There is only one road to democracy: education. And in a democracy, there is only one essential task for the educator: teaching liberty.[17]

The Moral Context

Liberty is a contextual concept. It conveys a sense of being unfettered: doors that open to the touch, no fences, no burdensome

restraints, no regulations. The more we add words that picture unbridled freedom, the more troublesome the concept becomes. It
leads to what Barry Bull calls "an embarrassment of riches" that
must be overcome if the individual pursuit of liberty is not to be
self-defeating.[18]

Bull argues that freedom must be limited when its exercise
would unreasonably interfere with that of others' freedoms. The
freedom to buy and sell other people, for example, must be re-
stricted; whereas the freedom to hold religious beliefs must not. But
the necessary distinctions are not always this easily made. It is somewhat easier to identify self-defeating freedoms—the equal exercise
of which by all members of society frustrates the very purpose of
the freedoms themselves—than it is to distinguish risk-laden freedoms—those that impede the freedoms of others only under certain circumstances.[19] It is easy to see that freedom to operate an
automobile without license or restraint is self-defeating. It is much
more difficult to argue that home schooling throughout the whole
of childhood and adolescence is risk-laden for the family. It is even
more difficult to argue that widespread home schooling is dangerous to the well-being of a democratic society. One can only make
the argument convincing when there is common recognition that
the aim of education is twofold: preparation for duties of citizenship and preparation to lead a good life.

Because there usually is implicit understanding of the personal,
individual nature of the educative process by those who seek to
define it, most definitions stress the second aim of the two, sometimes to complete omission of the first. And because this awareness
usually is accompanied by keen sensitivity to the corrupting of education through making it instrumental to all manner of political,
economic, and social purposes, care usually is taken to close the
door to such abuses.

There is, for example, very little room for narrowly conceived
contextual intrusions into Israel Scheffler's definition: "the formation of habits of judgment and the development of character, the
elevation of standards, the facilitation of understanding, the development of taste and discrimination, the stimulation of curiosity and
wondering, the fostering of style and a sense of beauty, the growth
of a thirst for new ideas and visions of the yet unknown."[20] Yet,
mostly for its omission of education as instrument to jobs, Scheffler's definition is regarded in some quarters as elitist and out of
sight for many. Mortimer Adler, on the other hand, simply yields to
popular perception and adds preparation for earning a living to the

dual aim of citizenship and self-realization.[21] Scheffler's "visions of the yet unknown" evokes images of cultivating the imagination, provoking the wrath of those who interpret this to mean the elevation of human reasoning over divine will. This objection then leads to further argumentation over whose god or whose interpretation of God shall prevail.

The sobering reality, already sharply put forward in the quotes from Barber, is that education and democracy are inextricably woven together. If there is an instrumentality here, it lies in the fact that each is instrumental to the other. Education must ritually take place in a democratic context; democracy must ritually resort to educational processes. Ends alone must never be used to justify means; all means must be justified in their own right, with moral principles outweighing all others. This is a perspective that counterbalances the unbridled pursuit of individual freedom. It is a perspective that currently runs counter to many of the most popular contingencies of American life. The issue is whether there can be some common center—some *unum*—where rational, moral concepts of freedom and responsibility, the essence of democracy, join divine law, the essence of religion, where the rough edges of secular and sectarian dogma fade into the shadows. What is the role of education in creating and expanding that center?

Clearly, it is a moral one that has little to do with behavioral doctrines and much to do with the circumstances of liberty.* The distinctions among political and social democracy and a democracy of humankind generate distinctions in the morality called for. Oakeshott denotes three idioms of moral condition: the morality of individuality, the morality of community ties, and the morality of the common good:

> In the morality of individuality, human beings are recognized . . . as separate and sovereign individuals. . . . Morality is the art of mutual accommodation. . . . In the morality of communal ties, human beings are recognized solely as members of a community and all activity whatsoever is understood to be communal activity. . . . This is an idiom of *moral* conduct, because the manner of this communal activity is, in fact, art and not nature. . . . The morality of the common good

---

*My colleagues and I have had a difficult time explaining that our use of "moral" in defining teaching, teacher education, and the conduct of schooling pertains to the conditions of sustaining settings in which freedom is experienced and exercised equally by all. We eschew indulging in a litany of behavioral oughts and shoulds—that is, moralizing.

springs from . . . the emergence of a different idiom of human character. Human beings are recognized as independent centers of activity,
but approval attaches itself to conduct in which this individuality is
suppressed whenever it conflicts, not with the individuality of others,
but with the interest of a "society" understood to be composed of such
human beings. All are engaged in a single, common enterprise. . . . and
morality is the art in which this condition is achieved and maintained.[22]

The arts of mutual accommodation, of communal ties, and of
the common good are teachable. These are the liberal arts of
Barber's educational imperative. They define a large part of what
education is: a deliberate, systematic, and sustained effort to develop
and refine human sensibilities and sensitivities.[23] Without it, democracy cannot be sustained.

The Immorality of Educational Denial

In Chapter 1, I discussed both the ubiquity and the power of education. Throughout history, tyrants and governments have endeavored to shut it down for some people. Given the plethora of media
today, this is more difficult to do than in any previous time. Nonetheless, there remain powerful ways, including those of the media,
to manipulate parts of the educational infrastructure so as to both
heighten their relevance to individual aspirations and regulate access.
This works to the advantage of a political régime of power.
Denial of the full development of selfhood through curtailing
access to education is, of course, immoral when viewed from the
perspective of what is right for humankind. But those seeking to
rule by power invariably seek simultaneously to reify much more
parochial norms that support their interests. They capture as much
as possible of the educational delivery system to inculcate these
norms so that they will come to be the guiding moral values. When
this is done successfully, they claim to rule not by the sword but by
the grace of God. Some terribly immoral things have been done in
the name of God.
Similarly, some terribly immoral things have been done in the
name of science. Over the past 150 years in particular, *biological
determinism* has had utility for individuals and groups in power on
a par with invoking deities: "It holds that shared behavioral norms,
and the social and economic differences between human groups—
primarily races, classes, and sexes—arise from inherited, inborn distinctions and that society, in this sense, is an accurate reflection of
biology."[24]

Invoking science to explain nature's sorting of human potential has provided more than an alternative to sorting attributed to God. Socrates turned to God as creator to justify the education and assignment of citizens to three classes: rulers, auxiliaries, and craftsmen. Today, he could cite scientific evidence and thus reify what earlier had to be accepted on faith. Stephen Jay Gould states the transformation wryly: "Millions of people are now suspecting that their social prejudices are scientific facts after all."[25] Unburdened by doubt, we can proceed with the distinctions among people our imperfect democracy perpetuates.

However, the unique American experiment with education and democracy may have made it easier for the nation's people to eschew doubt than to eschew guilt. Gunnar Myrdal envisioned that America could not live comfortably over the long haul with political inequality for African Americans based on assumed biological causation of inferiority.[26] James B. Conant referred to the nation's congenital deficiency—a part of her people enslaved—as contributing significantly to the growing urban unrest of his time.[27] There is hollowness and hypocrisy in the gulf between the celebration of one people born free and equal and a history of denying the education needed for full realization of selfhood on the basis of sex and race. What many people have trouble comprehending or do not want to comprehend is that the consequences of this denial redound to common as well as individual detriment. Social and political democracy are systemic; the existence of deprived individuals and groups in a culture is akin to the existence of deprived organs in a faltering human being.

The purpose of the public part of the educational infrastructure in a democracy is to ensure civicism in everyone so as to create, in turn, a *civitas* not unduly strained by unbridled individualism. This public purpose is not easily served under the best of circumstances. But when the necessary education is denied to some, the civil fabric is surely strained. The voice of punishment drowns out the voice of education.

Biological determinism has been used and continues to be used to authenticate opinions already formed out of prejudice and fear. Clearly, went the argument based on craniology, the claimed-to-be-larger cranium of white males over women and black males warranted a greater investment in and higher expectations for the education of white men. In 1879, Gustave Le Bon, a founder of social psychology, summed up the case against women:

All psychologists who have studied the intelligence of women, as well as poets and novelists, recognize today that they represent the most inferior forms of human evolution and that they are closer to children and savages than to an adult, civilized man. . . . A desire to give them the same education, and, as a consequence, to propose the same goals for them, is a dangerous chimera.[28]

Paul Broca, founder of the Anthropological Society of Paris, already had savaged people of black skin, male and female (1866):

A prognathous (forward-jutting) face, more or less black color of the skin, woolly hair and intellectual and social inferiority are often associated, while more or less white skin, straight hair and an orthognathous (straight) face are the ordinary equipment of the highest groups in the human series. . . . A group with black skin, woolly hair and a prognathous face has never been able to raise itself spontaneously to civilization.[29]

A colleague of Broca's, G. Hervé, administered the *coup de grâce* to women and black men simultaneously in 1881: "Men of the black races have a brain scarcely heavier than that of white women."[30]

Differences in brain weight (laboriously determined from cranial measurements) between races and sexes, equated with differences in intelligence, confirmed a priori conventional wisdom as scientific fact. Subsequent efforts to disprove the equation encountered hardened terrain. After all, conventional wisdom had assumed and taught all along that women and black men are intellectually inferior to white men. Scientific findings with respect to brain size merely provided one set of confirming facts among more yet to come. Even scientists of the time rejected the argument that the smaller size of women might account for smaller brain size but did not suggest lesser intelligence. Rather, the comparatively small size of the female brain results from a combination of both physical and intellectual inferiority! Needless to say, the scientific work cited in support of mischievous beliefs such as this was conducted by men.

There is no way to assess the consequences of such beliefs and the denial of education stemming from them on either the individuals so stereotyped or an entire nation. Certainly, the rise of teaching as a female occupation when women were not valued for intellect stunted its development as a profession and deprived it, ironically, of many of our brightest and most able men.[31] And the significant role of women today in business, communications, law, higher education, and the arts conveys a deep sense of what was lost before most of the veil regarding their inferiority was lifted.

The fact that only a corner of the veil has been lifted in regard to the assumed genetic inferiority of people of color bespeaks a tragedy of epic proportions. The use and abuse of intelligence tests in the 20th century[32] has replaced the measurement of heads in the 19th to sustain in part deep-seated prejudice and accompanying denial of access to knowledge and the full flowering of our democracy. Failure of the nation to see its best interests served through accelerating minority educational advancement supports Conant's observation of its having been born with a congenital deficiency that more than two centuries of rhetorical allegiance to democratic principles have failed to ameliorate.[33]

The use of biological determinism to justify unequal educational opportunity on the basis of sex and race has been assumed to be an ordering of human affairs according to the dictates of nature. Furthermore, social policy geared to the provision of education beyond the elementary school years has fit nicely with long-standing economic theory: A robust economy requires only that a portion of the people receive more advanced schooling.[34] Not everyone need be educated and, certainly, educational effort need not be geared to the abilities of those less able to benefit from it (i.e., women and minorities). The idea of investing in human capital as national wealth[35] is not new, but its time is not yet come. We should not be surprised, I suppose, that the idea of investing in education for all as a moral imperative for both the individual and the democratic state has little currency in much of economic theory. For many people, including a substantial percentage of our political leaders, views such as those expressed by the economist Friedrich A. von Hayek hold sway: "All societies have unequal wealth and income dispersion, and there is no positive basis for criticizing any degree of market determined inequality."[36] The concepts of education as a human right, the immorality of its denial, and the danger of this denial to a democratic society are viewed by many as strange, almost comical, idealism that has little place in the "real" world.

Individual Freedom and the Common Good

The single-minded pursuit of individualism—whether in the rational idiom with financial independence the goal, or through the canons of religious doctrine in seeking salvation of the soul—is the obverse of *communitas*. Mecca is a ghetto of one, from which choices of communication with other ghettos and of necessary support systems are carefully made. The demands on moral ethic and moral art are restrained and muted. Indeed, self-interest and conceptions of morality often are closely entangled.

A community driven by the economic ethic is a collection of semi-isolated individuals cherishing privacy and respecting each other's coming together to validate life's chase. A community driven by canons of individual salvation is an encampment of like-minded believers sustaining a common faith. Personal comfort and assurance depend on the absence of dissonance—any kind of dissonance. In the short history of the American democracy, we readily see the discomfort of immigrants now "settled" with the intrusion of newcomers of different languages, beliefs, customs, and colors. The moral arts that once sufficed are severely tested, as are education and the democracy that must support it.

Given the dissolution of many communal arrangements through the dissonance of fundamental human differences interacting over the centuries, what hope is there for democracy? And what might we expect from education, particularly in our unique democracy where we are given to join it with celebration of the self?

This is not the place for elaborate documentation of education's triumphs in the domains of both individual freedom and the common good. The evidence is all around us: in the courts' upholding of equity, in the contribution of the health sciences to human welfare, in the surge of learning to take care of our own bodies, in the steady march toward recognizing the rights of women and minorities, in adult testimony to primary grade teachers who fanned the sparks of their careers in human services, in deeds of sacrifice reported daily in the media. Anyone who has participated deeply over time in the conversation of adult seminars knows that profound changes in personality and world view are not the prerogative solely of the young. When education fails, it probably is falsely labeled.

Nonetheless, there is abundant, sobering evidence to the effect that immersion in circumstances designed to be educational provides no assurance that the desired results will occur. The record is replete with incidents of bright, much-schooled individuals who lie, cheat, steal, and kill. Some do so even after election to high office and commitments to be the nation's stewards. Graduates of our most prestigious schools and universities have brought their corporations to the brink of disaster and then blamed the public schools for economic malaise. We stand in awe over the incredible triumph of technology in transforming primitive dependence on natural forces to a large measure of control in just a few generations. And we are sickened by the human savagery and inhumanity that still abounds. Those who fear what education unleashes should fear more what education has not yet reached.

Our educational aims speak to extraordinary expectations for effecting the necessary transition from narcissistic selfhood to family, to community, to the whole of humankind—to habitual practice of the democratic moral arts. This self-transcendence requires a harmonious relationship between reason and faith in both the individual and the community. The canons of rationalism and the canons of religious doctrine and theocracy join in the language and presence of freedom, justice, civility, and *civitas*.

The democratic community cultivates the necessary language and behavior through ensuring education for all and freedom in religious belief. The voices of reason and of faith are not in the same mode and must not be confused. And yet, they must be respectful of one another and kept in balance, with the voices of fear, despair, and punishment muted.

Regarding reason, we turn to Philip Phenix:

> The rationalist faith is that there is one standpoint—that of disciplined reason—which comprehends all the others, making it possible to escape the relativities of time and culture and the illusions of provincialism. This is the peculiar property of reason, that it enables man to achieve a degree of universality, to rise to some extent above the limitations of circumstance and history.[37]

Regarding religion, we read the words of Warren Wagar:

> Each of the higher religions sees divinity from its own special point of view, but . . . all agree that man is not the greatest spiritual presence in the universe, and needs contact and union with the higher spiritual reality beyond the phenomena of sense experience or physical theory. They differ in their holy places, rituals, taboos, social conventions, myths, and theological systems, but the openhearted behavior, by disengaging the nonessentials from the essentials in mankind's religious heritage, can find a common core of truth in all the positive religions.[38]

On reason and religion, again from Wagar:

> In true religion the ultimate reality is a transcendental being, power, or principle. But . . . the same search for final meaning can be pur-

sued in much the same way by secular religions, or ideologies. . . . The nation, or a given social order, or a type of humanity, is divinized.[39]

There is a center, then, where the two major themes that have driven human existence come together, where one supports without seeking to preempt the other. This evolving center, never static, takes on a cultural sacredness, a "sense of interconnections among the individual, the collectivity, and ultimate purpose and meaning of human existence."[40] The American democracy is in urgent need of more than a rhetorical surge of sensitivity and sensibility regarding the significance and necessity of this core.

Benjamin Barber sees the educational process of self-transcendence that should be a large part of the school's business overwhelmed by the contingencies of the marketplace and the self-selected ghetto: "We honor ambition, we reward greed, we celebrate materialism, we worship acquisitiveness, we cherish success, and we commercialize the classroom—and then we bark at the young about the gentle art of the spirit."[41]

This problem of contextual malaise is ever-present in a society of such devotion to individualism. Sarason argues, however, that there was once "a time when it was literally impossible for people to separate belief in a divinity from the sense of belonging to a geographically circumscribed human community."[42] The modern world, he writes, has severed these two needs through impoverishing the ties that bind one to a human community. Many people—including the much-schooled and economically successful—no longer possess the psychological sense of community even if they do not or cannot give up the need for transcendence through belief in a divinity.[43] Out of losing or fear of losing community, they often become obsessed with belief.

This phenomenon is not new to our culture. A hundred and fifty years ago, Alexis de Tocqueville wrote about the restlessness of Americans in the midst of their prosperity.

> It is odd to watch with what feverish ardor the Americans pursue prosperity and how they are ever tormented by the shadowy suspicion that they may not have chosen the shortest route to get it. . . . It seemed to me that . . . they seemed serious and almost sad in their pleasures.[44]

But then he observed that

> there are momentary respites when their souls seem suddenly to break the restraining bonds of matter and rush impetuously heavenward. In

every state of the Union . . . there are preachers hawking the word of God from place to place. Whole families, old men, women, and children cross difficult country and make their way through untamed forests to come great distances to hear them. Here and there throughout American society you meet men filled with an enthusiastic, almost fierce spirituality such as cannot be found in Europe. From time to time strange sects arise which strive to open extraordinary roads to eternal happiness. Forms of religious madness are very common there.[45]

Tocqueville said that we should not be surprised at this, basing his argument on the compelling needs of the soul. Sarason argues somewhat differently. Admitting to the need for transcendence through belief in a divinity, he would see the human sadness to which Tocqueville referred arising out of today's loss of a sense of community. And in the resulting psychological stress, I see fear with all of its concomitant dangers.

Making Democracy Safe for Education

The fear I fear stems from twin tensions always present in democracy that are not easily kept in balance. One of these twins is in the balance between individual freedom and the restraints required to prevent a community from reverting to anarchy and endangering everyone's freedom. The unbridled, narcissistic pursuit of freedom we see all around us is powerfully contagious and, ultimately, self-defeating. If the traffic lights at all intersections were removed, we might rejoice for a little while in the freedom of driving through them as creatively as we wished. But this exercise of self-defeating freedom would soon lead to destruction, fear, and mayhem.

The other twin tension grows out of the very diversity democracy must protect. Diversity places great demands on tolerance, another democratic virtue. Just when I have become comfortable with the classical, I am confronted with modernism and postmodernism. Just as I am becoming accepting of the lifestyle next door to me, the two men propose marriage and the adoption of a child. The church and the synagogue exist quite comfortably side by side in the community, but the mosque now rising toward the heavens is creating dissonance. Just as I begin to think that our elected leaders are coming to understand the public purpose of schooling, another school board trusts the management of its schools to a private corporation. Enough already. The freedom democracy seeks to cultivate and protect appears to be running ahead of the community that must nurture it.

Accepting Barber's observation that democracy is "an extraordinary and rare contrivance of cultivated imagination," we must give constant attention to all existing and potentially educative contingencies. Some 1,000 to 1,200 hours of schooling each year for the young do not suffice. Nor will extending these hours to 1,500 or so each year—as is frequently proposed—be sufficient. Schools alone cannot do the necessary educating, even if their public purpose were understood and vigorously supported. But the ongoing struggle for the soul of the American public school currently is focused on its private purpose. The more school time is devoted to private purpose at the expense of public purpose, the less likely it is that schools will contribute their share to the learning of the democratic arts. With the democratic moral arts neglected in the common school (or in schools grown uncommon), the likelihood of its graduates creating *civitas* declines.

The irony is that schools require the context of a civil society in order to perform well their public, democratic purpose. The American tendency to equate education and schooling and make schools the instrument for satisfying our wants and alleviating our malaise takes attention from our circumstances. We beat on schools, leaving the contextual circumstances unaddressed. Schools can neither bring back the geographically circumscribed community to which Sarason refers nor satisfy the diversity of sectarian beliefs in a divinity that the call for the teaching of "family values" so often disguises. But they can contribute to the traits students must develop if they are to replace the lost geographic community with a civil society that respects, among other freedoms, one's right to sectarian beliefs. Barber observed:

> Civil society is a societal dwelling place that is neither a capital building nor a shopping mall. It shares with the private sector the gift of liberty; it is voluntary and is constituted by freely associating individuals and groups. But unlike the private sector, it aims at common ground and consensual, integrative, and collaborative action. Civil society is thus public without being coercive, voluntary without being private.[46]

The toughest problems to be encountered in the sustenance of civil societies simply are those of sustaining a robust democracy. They are essentially those of drawing in people from the periphery to ensure a sufficient mass of inclusion. On one hand is that segment of the citizenry that has virtually isolated itself from everything counter to near-independent tenets of individualism, and on the other is that larger segment of vulnerable individuals and groups whose isolation is not of choice but of disadvantage and prejudice. The civil society renews in part through its success in drawing more and more of those on the periphery into belief in and practice of the moral dispositions it values. It does this primarily through its educative infrastructure, much of it participatory, and through the laws thought necessary to the control of self-defeating freedoms.

These laws are obligatory, not because they are laws of nature or laid down by God, but because they have been made, promulgated, and interpreted through democratic processes with a view to keeping the peace. In the vein of Hobbes, they are civil laws.[47] Improvement of the human condition depends on widespread recognition of and adherence to these laws, the making of enlightened public policy, sound social engineering to implement policies, and continuing attention to the material needs of the citizenry. The need for such laws grows less with maturation of the civil society, but the never-ending tension between individualism and the commonweal necessitates their continuing presence.

Secular and Spiritual Morality

I have referred to three democracies—of government, community, and the human spirit—and the moral arts that sustain them. The moral arts of the civil community, of the common good, appear rooted in the human idiom. On the surface, they appear more secular than spiritual. Consequently, they appear to be insufficient for the intentions and dispositions of all those individuals necessary to the civil society. Much of the tension in the American democracy that surfaces (particularly over the education schools are to provide) concerns secular versus spiritual morality—over morality in the human or the divine idiom. Often, argument comes down to a standoff over whether and what values are to be taught.

Given the materialism described by Barber and the conflict among strongly held concepts of morality, what hope is there of our schools' being able to serve the public purpose of developing civic responsibility in a democratic human community? Surely not by asking them to be morally vacuous, as many people are now doing. And surely not by charging them with strengthening sectarian faith, as others are doing. There must be a compatible union of the two kinds of transcendence.

The answer lies, I think, in understanding the nature of education and spreading this understanding throughout our communities. Those of us who are at least supposed to be well educated have a special responsibility to be a major part of this educational voice. We must hold steadfastly to the concept of education being inseparably moral.

We must help young and old to understand that education is development of the wisdom that defines selfhood and smoothes the self-transcendence that is rooted in community "and a sense of place in the past, present, and future of the human race."[48] As stated in Chapter 1, since wisdom has to do with the kinds of choices we make, wisdom is a moral concept. Education, then, is a moral undertaking. Consequently, teaching that seeks to go beyond the simplest rote learning is a moral endeavor.

This is a frightening idea for many people, particularly those suffering psychological stress and experiencing fear because of their own loss of or failure to gain a secure sense of place in humankind. If, in fear, we hobble the schools in the development of wisdom in their students, we might as well close them and permit instruction to go on unrestrained by the controls we can properly place on our schools and teachers. Teaching the young is an incredibly risk-laden responsibility. We must be sure that a large part of it is done by wise, caring parents who understand the nature of education and by teachers who have experienced the best in liberal and professional studies in universities and in the exemplary schools with which such institutions must be in partnership.

In advancing the concept of education and teaching as moral endeavors,[49] my colleagues and I understand the trouble some people have with that much used and abused word *moral*. They tend to equate it with sectarian litanies of "thou shalt" and "thou shalt not" and raise the question of whose litanies are to be taught. What we have in mind, rather, is education that develops in humans the dispositions to make choices that benefit self and community mutually.

The British philosopher, John White, believes there to be moral dispositions that should be acceptable to all people in a democratic society: fairness, equality, justice, freedom, caring, community, and relatedness.[50] The public purpose of schooling in a democratic society should be the teaching of those altruistic dispositions that cultivate the transcendent self in the democratic community. Thus the voice of reason and hope is sustained and nurtured. Democracy is made safer for the education in schools democracy needs.

But what about the voice of faith? The fascinating thing is that all these temporally derived dispositions ultimately merge with those spiritually derived in the world's major religions. After careful study, Warren Wagar concludes:

> All the formulas for the spiritual unification of man converge in perfect harmony. . . . They all affirm and reverence life; they all believe in the freedom and integrity of the person; they all urge the existential self to seek self-transcendence in organic union with mankind and with mystical or divine ground of the cosmos; and they all discover the spiritual resources for human effort in the power of unconditional love. About these four final values—life, personality, transcendence, and love—there is no disagreement whatever in nearly the whole range of contemporary prophetic literature.[51]

His conceptual union of the terrestrial and the spiritual aligns with the vision of the Founding Fathers in their forging of the Constitution of the United States of America. The common principles are recognized in our civil law and under God. Yet, many people have lost or seen not their sacredness and have grown fearful. The American democracy is approaching crisis not only because the voice of punishment born of this fear is on the rise but also because the altruistic dispositions it needs for its renewal are being drowned in the troubled waters of excessive secular narcissism and sectarian dogmatism.

Surely there are enough of us among the most-schooled people in the world who have wisdom enough and faith enough to turn us around and avoid the dire prediction made by British philosopher Olaf Stapledon more than six decades ago:

> The first, and some would say the greatest, achievement of . . . "Western" culture was the conceiving of two ideals of conduct, both essential to the spirit's well-being. Socrates, delighting in the truth for its own sake and not merely for practical ends, glorified unbiased thinking, honesty of mind and speech. Jesus, delighting in the actual human persons around him, and in that flavour of divinity which, for him, pervaded the world, stood for unselfish love of neighbours and of God. . . . Socrates urged intellectual integrity, Jesus integrity of will. Each, of course, though starting with a different emphasis, involved the other.
> Unfortunately both these ideals demanded of the human brain a degree of vitality and coherence of which the . . . First Men [were] never really capable. . . . And the failure to put these ideals in practice helped to engender in the race a cynical lassitude which was one cause of its decay.[52]

Knowing the road to take, have we not the integrity of intellect urged by Socrates and the integrity of will urged by Jesus? The voices of hope and faith must teach that we do. The twin voices of education and religion must lead us beyond our enervating, debilitating divisiveness to a social democracy of the human spirit that transcends individualism and binds humankind—somewhere a place for all of us, together. In both our temporal and our spiritual houses there must be many mansions.

CHAPTER 3

Education and Community

The preceding chapter spoke of loss in the human condition and its consequences. This loss is of ties that bind, that lodge the self securely and comfortably in social contexts, both geographic and of the human conversation. Sarason referred to the loss as a dual one—of a geographically circumscribed community on one hand and of a sense of belonging through a shared core of beliefs on the other. The consequences include a hunkering down, fear, and distrust. One's scope of interactions and values shared with others shrinks.

The above is descriptive of a present condition that appears to be growing in intensity. The sphere of close human engagement has been narrowing simultaneously with an expansion in casual, impersonal relationships. The recorded message concludes with the admonition, "Have a nice day." The telephoned effort to secure one's bank balance goes to an unidentifiable source and, in time, to recorded information regarding the button to push, recorded music, and, in still more time, perhaps the answer. Money spent on electronics has replaced money spent on employees to the extent that the clients to be served now spend more time (unpaid) performing services once provided by paid humans. Money thus saved now must go to intensified electronically driven public relations efforts designed to attract and hold clients—even though studies show that the greatest of the many grievances people now have with banks, for example, is disappearance of the human connection. Frustration builds, to be released elsewhere.

The 20th century has been marked throughout by rapid changes in the context of daily life and the demands placed upon humans to adjust. Schools have been called upon again and again to provide the mechanisms of adjustment signaled by changing prefixes to the word *education*: vocational education, economic education, air age education, new era education, computer education, or the all-encompassing life adjustment education. The schools have come through again and again—or at least have been credited with such. But schools get credit and appear to succeed when the human condition surrounding them is buoyant and healthy, when social capital is widely shared and the gap between the financial capital of the haves and have-nots appears not to be egregiously obscene. In effect, there is optimism even in the face of rapid change of great potential when there is a solid core of middle-class resilience, with many people well prepared to take advantage of what appear to be benefits to come.

Clearly, there are potential benefits in the electronic revolution now taking place. Much-schooled, strategically placed individuals in both the corporate and academic work force have at their disposal the equivalent of services only recently available to senior executives and successful grant-getters and the independence that goes with such. For self-transcending, secure individuals, grounded in many layers of the human conversation, the loss of the personal in the marketplace serves primarily to remind them that the times are changing. Environments characterized by anonymity are a boon to fast-track individualism; there is no demand for or loss of time in friendly conversation. But for growing numbers of the displaced and vulnerable now at the margins of participation, uncertainty and fear prevail over hope.

The electronic, new-wave revolution might be just one more to be absorbed and managed if there were a solid infrastructure of well-connected communities, each with the necessary services, safety nets, and decision-making processes in place so that the decentralization of work and other daily activity could take place in orderly fashion. Instead, the number of little encampments with attitudes of "going it alone" increases, at the same time that communities of common economic and sometimes common professional interests but no circumscribed geographic base are on the rise. The grange and town hall as places of discussion and action for the common good have almost withered away. Robert Putnam, noting the decline in bowling teams, uses "Bowling Alone" metaphorically in his analysis of a downward spiral of civic engagement.[1]

Toward What Communities?

The certainties of tomorrow will likely differ from rather than be the same as the certainties we have had or known in the past.

The future's commonalities with the past will be fewer. Yet, they must be more commonly and deeply held and practiced if tomorrow's story of humankind is to be at least as uplifting as yesterday's. There is no point in seeking nostalgically to tie to yesterday's anchors; many of them are fathoms deep under shifting sands. Yet, we must find equivalents that simultaneously secure the individual and the polity liberty requires. The contingencies are those that assist individuals to self-transcend toward broad participation in the human conversation which increasingly will transcend circumscribed geographic boundaries. These contingencies are educative ones. Terrestrial grounding alone will not suffice.

I use "participation in the human conversation" as a metaphor for the whole of living: in the family, at school, at work and play, in civic engagement, in appreciating the arts, in conserving what future generations will require, in contemplation, in comprehending the miracle and sanctity of life, in creating healthy conditions for all humans. In Chapter 2, I took a stand with respect to what I believe the healthy human condition to be: self-transcendence from early childhood narcissism, to sustenance and growth in the family, to secure giving and receiving in civil communities stretching from neighborhood to humankind, with altruism the mark of maturity. Ideally, there is no giving up of one stage for the next; indeed, what one carries to the next are the benefits from where one has been. Similarly, blemishes in an early stage, such as child abuse in the family, compound self-transcendence to and in the next. The danger signals are in reifying the assumed virtues of an early stage of the self-transcendent process so that they become the standard for practicing and judging the moral arts. If the standard of morality is mutual accommodation in the context of the family and extends no further outward, the prospects for a civil society are dim.

In Chapter 2, I cited Stephen Jay Gould's wry observation on conventional wisdom derived from the misinterpretation of research: "Millions of people are now suspecting that their social prejudices are scientific facts after all." Now we have a parallel based on political validation: Many people are having an easy time of it in regard to social consciousness because family values provide the standard for the moral arts. Career politicians have found rhetoric designed to blunt growing citizen concern over seemingly unresponsive government in far-off places. They work and rework the theme of "family values," leaving the listener to fill in the blanks with whatever beliefs and actions she or he wishes justified. The absence of definition and specification serve both political and individual purpose. William Bennett's *The Book of Virtues*[2] received a polite reception but stirred no consensus-seeking among the most vocal advocates of family values. Bennett's comprehensive list left no room for the justification of child neglect and wife beating.

There is a kind of mischievousness about the simultaneous political exhortation of family values and the need to get government out of people's daily lives. With values not defined, it leaves to individuals freedom that, unenlightened by contingencies designed to reinforce the communal moral arts, readily becomes self-defeating. Ironically, the political spotlighting of family values creates uneasiness for those people who most cherish the sanctity and privacy of the family and would resent any effort to specify "correct" dispositions. Fortunately, all those who are rightly shocked by the political exploitation taking place can take heart from the degree to which cartoonists and satirists draw attention to the glass houses of some of the most sanctimonious advocates of family values. A shift to new slogans will soon follow.

Unfortunately, changing shifts in political attention often bear no connection to community need. The resolution of malaise depends heavily on the smallest units of the infrastructure. These must join in a collectivity of spirit and action. Sole reliance on the family as the unit of providing and caring leads in the opposite direction. The acquisition of altruistic dispositions in a supportive family is a critically important step in self-transcendence, but it is not the top step of the staircase.

Symbiotics and Symbioses

"Politics is the art of associating men for the purpose of establishing, cultivating, and conserving social life among them. Whence it is called 'symbiotics.'"[3] So wrote Johannes Althusius—whose work currently is stirring interest in several scholarly fields—four centuries ago. For Althusius, "symbiosis" is living together. For him, symbiotics and symbiosis include all human associations. There was little ambiguity in the symbiotics and symbiosis Althusius prescribed for the family:

> There are . . . common advantages and responsibilities that are provided and communicated by both spouses, such as kindness, use of the body for avoiding harlotry and for procreating children, mutual habitation except when absence may be necessary, intimate and familiar companionships, mutual love, fidelity, patience, mutual service,

communication of all goods and rights, . . . management of the family, administration of household duties, education of children in the true religion, protection against and liberation from perils, and mourning of the dead.[4]

From this base of what he defines as natural association, Althusius moves outward to the civil association he calls "The Collegium," which is a body organized to serve a common utility and necessity in human life. In this context, the family role is transcended to be replaced by that of an ally and citizen. But the mutuality stressed for the family is necessarily sustained:

> Mutual benevolence is that affection and love of individuals toward their colleagues because of which they harmoniously will and "nill" on behalf of the common utility. The benevolence is nourished, sustained, and conserved by public banquets, entertainments, and love feasts.[5]

Prescriptions for the art and practice of human associations are then extended to "the collegium of wise and select men to whom are entrusted the affairs of the city,"[6] and ultimately the whole of secular and ecclesiastical communication. The same fundamental principles of justice, civility, fairness, and caring pertain. One does not give up the symbiotics and symbioses appropriate to what might be termed virtuous family life. But they are left in and to the home. Other moral democratic arts must be learned for the symbiotics and symbioses beyond the family.

Throughout the several editions of his book *Politica*, Althusius develops a central theme pertaining to the basic nature of humans which is, for me, of critical importance in considering the role of education and schooling, a theme that I pick up specifically in Chapter 4. In Chapter 1, I argued that a public purpose for education geared to the economic marketplace could not be sustained over time, simply because such does not encompass the full nature of humankind—neither Scheffler's conception of the individual's "thirst for new ideas and visions of the yet unknown" nor Althusius's conception of "symbiotic man":*

> The end of political "symbiotic" man is holy, just, comfortable, and happy symbiosis, a life lacking nothing either necessary or useful. Truly, in liv-

---

*One must remember the 16th- and 17th-century context of Johannes Althusius in seeking to cope with many of his assumptions regarding the God-given status of men as head of the household and in all public matters.

ing this life no man is self-sufficient, or adequately endowed by nature. . . . Bereft of all counsel and aid, for which nevertheless he is then in greatest need, he is unable to help himself without the intervention and assistance of another. . . . Therein he is called upon to perform those virtues that are necessarily inactive except in this symbiosis.[7]

Robinson Crusoe craved companionship to ease his lonely life. It is interesting to note how quickly after encountering Friday he contaminated the potential. The civil arts of the culture in which Crusoe had grown up dictated the "proper" relationship to be established with the "colored" man. Crusoe lost no time in dubbing his new-found servant his "Man Friday." Millions of schoolchildren and their teachers have viewed this conferring of status to be entirely appropriate. One's culture is a profoundly impactful teacher.

Expanding the Symbiotic Circle

What civil communities of the future will require is not just the small symbiotic units conveyed by the words *family values* but successively larger ones held together by communal values, with *communal* writ large. This does not mean disavowing family values but, rather, extending the symbiotic principles to an interlocking array of larger entities. The dispositions that serve the former well are essentially those that serve the latter well. This is not, however, a matter of fitting, Procrustean-like, the morality of community ties to the morality of the individual family. Rather, it means that the dispositions of fairness, equality, caring, relatedness, and the like, relevant to both community and family, are learned. These are relevant to all associations, be they of family, friends, or the citizenry and be they ecclesiastical or secular.

Robert Bellah and his associates, in prescribing for friendship associations, drew upon the same sources and symbiotic concepts Althusius recommended for all human associations some four centuries earlier:

> The conception of friendship put forward by Aristotle, elaborated by Cicero, and understood for centuries in the context of the Christian conception of personhood . . . had three essential components. Friends must enjoy one another's company, they must be useful to one another, and they must share a common commitment to the good.[8]

Edward Banfield (1958) reported case data on a village in southern Italy that might be described as dead with respect to association beyond the individual family. As Walter Parker cites Banfield's findings: "There was no organized action whatsoever in the face of severe local problems. Locals complained bitterly about them, but they did nothing. There was no hospital, no newspaper, only five grades of school, no charities or welfare programs, no agricultural organization."[9]

Banfield called this *amoral familism* and hypothesized the following:

1. In a society of amoral familists, no one will further the interest of the group or community except as it is to his private advantage to do so.
2. In a society of amoral familists, only officials will concern themselves with public affairs, for only they are paid to do so.
3. In a society of amoral familists, there will be few checks on officials, for checking on officials will be the business of other officials only.
4. In a society of amoral familists, organization (i.e., deliberately concerted action) will be very difficult to achieve and maintain.[10]

Banfield implies a point that is critically important to any discussion of both social and political democracy. It is virtually impossible for even quite primitive communal life to function in the absence of an infrastructure designed to take care of a modicum of essential services. Without an interest in the conduct of these affairs, they are left to bureaucrats. Without an interest in monitoring the bureaucrats, this function, too, is taken over by other bureaucrats, with all the accompanying malaise of such arrangements. When people do not engage in civic behavior, they not only do not learn the moral arts of *communitas*, they lose the opportunity to learn them. The scope of their participation in the human conversation is curtailed.

The inquiry conducted by Robert Putnam and his colleagues not only places the above observation in a much larger context but also throws a great deal of light on what makes democratic institutions stable and effective. They studied two decades of the Italian experiment in regional representative government inaugurated in 1970, providing unusual and very rich documentation of connections between political and social democracies—symbiotics and symbioses. Putnam compares the histories of north and south and their differing legacies of citizens' participation in government and civic affairs. Over the centuries, Italy was dominated hierarchically in the south by a landed aristocracy with feudal powers, the church, and the Mafia. In contrast, by the 14th century a "fertile communal republicanism" was taking shape in the north.[11] These differing traditions profoundly differentiated the conduct of government and civic engagement in the regions and towns of the north from those of the south following the 1970 provision for creation of local governments. Putnam's research team found correlations between citizens' engagement in politics and their involvement in a wide variety of civic affairs that rather sharply contrasted northern regions such as Emilia-Romagna, scoring high, with southern regions such as Calabria, scoring lower, on their criteria of civicness.

> In the most civic regions, such as Emilia-Romagna, citizens are involved in all sorts of local associations—literary guilds, local banks, hunting clubs, cooperatives and so on. They follow civic affairs avidly in the local press, and they engage in politics out of programmatic conviction. By contrast, in the least civic regions, such as Calabria, voters are brought to the polls not by issues, but by hierarchical patron-client networks. An absence of civic associations and a paucity of local media in these latter regions mean that citizens there are rarely drawn into community affairs.[12]

Part of Putnam's analysis is of the effectiveness of government institutions. Beginning with the assumption that a good democratic government is both responsible to and effective in acting on the demands of its citizenry, he developed rigorous criteria for evaluating institutional performance. Putnam was able to establish high internal consistency among his 12 diverse indicators of institutional performance: "Regions that have stable cabinets, adopt their budgets on time, spend their appropriations as planned, and pioneer new legislation are, for the most part, the same regions that provide day care centers and family clinics, develop comprehensive urban planning, make loans to farmers, and answer their mail promptly.[13] And these were, for the most part, the regions with a legacy of civic-mindedness and civic participation.

Putnam observes that, in a civic community, citizens regard the public domain as something other than a battleground for pursuing personal interests. But he warns against ignoring the powerful motivation of self-interest. As stated earlier, the challenge is to bring about a symbiotic relationship between self-interest and community need. In today's world, this is not easy. Even when civic-mindedness is present, self-interest creates different images of the community to be sustained. At one extreme is that nostalgic ideal of one that blends God, family, neighborhood, town, and country in some modern reincarnation of a sacred core of meaning regained. At another, is a cosmopolitan view of my city linked to cities world-wide in a community of technological innovation and economic competition.

The coexistence of these extremes adds to the burdens of civic-mindedness. Putnam's descriptions of the functioning community appear to accommodate quite comfortably the first of these two visions. But it is the second that now seems to be growing in the civic-minded north he describes, especially among the young lead-ership that views itself as more commercially entrepreneurial than political. The increasingly powerful Northern League views the south as Italy's cumbersome baggage, Milan as their capital, and that city joined with other city-states, such as Paris, London, New York, Los Angeles, and Tokyo, engaged in global commerce that transcends nationhood.[14] What is the meaning of and the poten-tial for civicness and the moral arts of democracy under these circumstances?

Is the social glue that holds people together the same for na-tions, city-states, and small communities? Wallace Loh argues that it is:

> What holds us together is a commitment to certain core values that define our national identity and undergird our common purpose. These values include liberties of the mind, the freedom of inquiry and ex-pression essential to an open society; tolerance for intellectual and human differences; respect for individual dignity; fair process and equal treatment; mutual caring, a sense of responsibility for the com-mon good. Some of the values are found in the Constitution precisely because its framers recognized that they are fundamental civic virtues that make possible cooperative living in an interdependent society. These values are learned.[15]

Learned Sensitivities and Sensibilities

"These values are learned." Education one more time: the al-ternative to all of humankind's other ways for settling differences and disagreements and for advancing civilization. Not the instru-ment, the alternative. In the second of Laurens van der Post's pair of novels about a period of tumultuous change from the Africa he had known as a child, the young hero, François Joubert, hears the voice of his dead father:

It was only by education and re-education and patient exhortation and evocation and change of heart and imagination that men could be permanently changed. You could not punish men into being better; you could not punish societies into being more; you could not change the world by violence and by frightening people into virtue by killing off their inadequate establishments. The moment was upon us when we had to accept without reserve that the longest way round in the human spirit was always the shortest way there.[16]

What François heard his father reject remains both cause and effect in humankind's repertoire of ways to settle differences. How is the educational alternative to prevail? Becoming a nation much-schooled is, sadly, not sufficient. In the United States, we have compulsory schooling to the age of 16, one of the highest secondary school graduation rates in the world, and a comprehensive system of higher education that is the envy of most other nations. Yet, statistics regarding violence to one another are shocking, and cults espousing racial intolerance find ardent recruits among graduates of our most elite universities. Good marks in school predict good marks in school but not, it seems, later performance of the democratic moral arts.

Before we rise mindlessly to blame the school once more, we should ask ourselves whether we should be surprised. We no longer cultivate expectations for the public, democratic purpose of schools, nor do we engage in conversations regarding such. Fenstermacher points to both silence in regard to connecting education and democracy and myopia in regard to the ideals of education in the rhetoric of school reform:

> We hear a great deal about readying the next generation of workers for global competition, about being first in the world in such high status subjects as math and science, and about having world class standards for what is learned in school. We hear almost nothing about civic participation or building and maintaining democratic communities, whether these be neighborhoods or governments at the local, state or federal level. . . . Not only does the current national reform movement in the United States pay too little attention to the ideas and ideals of democracy, it pays far too little attention to the ideas and ideals of education.[17]

But even if we articulate school goals and programs for all three of Oakeshott's idioms of moral condition—the morality of individuality, of community, and of the common good (Chapter 2)—the values and daily activities of the marketplace would overwhelm the best that schools can do to civilize the young. Our obsession with the notion of schools as instruments for achieving our varied wants, given their good performance, has helped to dull us to the fragility of democracy and to the need for all of its citizens and agencies to sustain it. We can say repeatedly that education must not be equated with schooling only to have the assumption that they are one and the same confirmed the moment we catch our breath.

Lawrence Cremin once raised and answered the question of how the proper creation and education of a public balanced between individualism and community is to be achieved: We talk. But we have not the time, not the settings, and not the skills. When we talk, we prefer to tell and tend to do it in settings and situations where response is not expected or easily given. We listen poorly, rarely converse, and eschew disciplined conversation. In a world where workers increasingly are in the domain labeled communications, the neglected learning is the art of civil discourse.

Television's sitcoms always elicit laughs out of the oft-repeated scenes of the family morning rush. Breakfast-cereal advertisements hardly ever show members of a family gathered at the table. Both the sitcoms and the advertisements reflect only too well the familiar. There is little parent-parent and parent-child conversation throughout the week. Many studies show that the family dinner hour has virtually disappeared, with members eating at different times and in different places. It was at the evening dinner table that the day's events were reviewed in the context of the family values embedded in my childhood and youth. This conversational ritual provided a large part of the social capital I brought to school. Today, writes Barber, "we bark at the young about the gentle art of the spirit" (Chapter 2).

There has not been, for me, any place outside the family, either as child or parent, that has offered equivalent degrees of freedom and unconditional love. There I learned much of what should not be said or done in public—outside of the very special privacy of the family. Beyond the vocational realm, there was no need to escape the "stifling" family restraints so often ascribed to family. Indeed, the potential freedoms likely to be offered on the outside usually carried with them the danger of being self-defeating. Reacting, apparently, to experience similar to mine, Fenstermacher argues that we need to pay more attention to strengthening family associations because it is through these that the morality of individuality is learned, and it is on this base that the moralities of community and the common good are built. "The time has come," he wrote, "when educators who grasp the essential links between education and democracy must extend their arguments and their visions beyond the schools and into homes. . . . For it is only when these domains of the private are healthy and vigorous that we may reasonably expect the schools to be successful in the work of education and democracy."[18]

More than three decades ago, Benjamin Bloom drew upon his review of more than a thousand studies in drawing a seminal conclusion about the degree to which cognition matures in the early years of life and, therefore, the significance of early childhood education.[19] There is no reason to believe that these years and, consequently, the family context are any less impactful in shaping the traits of mutuality and altruism the moral life requires. To speak of a democracy without them is to speak of an empty shell. In the words of Donna Kerr, "If persons live in relationships of domination and subservience, no rhetoric of democracy can render their relations democratic. Thus, even hopeful talk of schooling for civility disregards the moral character of democracy, namely that democracy pertains to how we human beings *are* with and toward one another."[20] Similarly, the pious exhortation of family values is meaningless as an ideal when there is neither civil conversation nor civil association in the family—and few contingencies deliberately directed to the sustenance of both. There is now no assurance that children will come to school with the social building blocks for this next phase of developing the sensitivities and sensibilities that come with the hoped-for transition from narcissism. David Elkind sums up a characteristic of the postmodern family as contrasted with the disappearing modern family:

> In keeping with the new sentiments of the permeable family, a new value has emerged. . . . This new value is *autonomy*, whereby each family member pursues his or her interests and puts these interests before those of the family. In the modern family, where togetherness reigned, having meals together took precedence over individual pursuits. Today, soccer practice, music lessons, and business meetings take precedence over sharing mealtimes. If the nuclear home was a haven, the permeable home is more like a busy railway station with people coming in for rest and sustenance before moving out on another track.[21]

Then, of course, there are homes where some family members never show up for a rest, as well as children and families that have no home to rest in. There is no question that creating havens of resting, sharing, and caring is one of the most critical and challenging problems of our time. The celebration of democracy without them is a myopic sham.

Sensitive critics have argued that there is no point in spending time and energy on schools—and especially on their public purpose—when so much of our political and social infrastructure is in disarray. But much of their criticism is directed penetratingly to the disarray and not to the myriad difficult steps that must be taken to ensure reasonably safe, healthy, productive, enjoyable lives for most people. I use the words *reasonably* and *most people* because higher expectations placed alongside of many discouraging realities have served not to inspire but to produce greater disillusionment. In reference to less daunting circumstances, I have quoted Alexander Pope's sardonic admonition in urging that we keep our expectations high: "Blessed is the man who expects nothing, for he shall never be disappointed."

In the light of human history, the prospect of ensuring reasonably good lives for most people is a very high expectation to be achieved, we must hope, within a generation. The prospect of a very good life for all is an idealistic expectation for the long term. The arena of action is civic space filled with reflective activity—civic space in which most everyone, young and old, is both teacher and learner.

Toward Educative Communities

Throughout the foregoing, I have referred explicitly to or implied the importance to humankind of an educative process through which individuals transcend the normal narcissism of the early years to become dispositionally and associationally altruistic. Robert Ulich described this as self-transcendence, with each stage building on without destroying or countering the previous one.[22] The dispositions and habits of moral choice do not change in kind; they are refined to serve in successively new and broader contexts. There is kinship in the theory of Althusius and that of Ulich 350 years later.

Implied are life phases, each providing a different context: family, institutions such as school, geographically prescribed community, state or nation, world, and universe. The transition is not made successfully through depending entirely on previous learnings; the parochial associations may broaden but there is no advance in universality. There is nothing inherently wrong or negative about dwelling forevermore at this plateau. Indeed, most of the good citizens who are honored for their community services are those whose ambitions and circumstances did not move them to a larger context. Some of those who have gone on in the cycle of self-transcendence become so preoccupied with the world beyond their local communities that they give little to them; maintaining the community infrastructure is left to others. Democratic communities from the smallest to the largest require a critical mass of individuals who have transcended to the point of acquiring the moral arts essential to the needs of the particular context. This is a kind of social capital acquired from the educative contingencies that are sustained. The absence of this social capital places a community in peril, be it family, school, neighborhood, state, or nation.

The essence of democratic communities is a multiplicity of occupations and preoccupations existing comfortably side by side, none dominant, with a multiplicity of horizontal connections and relationships among them. In order for individuals to pursue their particular interests, it is essential that there be in place an array of mechanisms that function smoothly and efficiently to provide basic human needs for health, transportation, safety, and the like. When the infrastructure of services breaks down, liberty is impaired. One must now engage in tasks of self-survival for which many are ill-prepared and probably disinterested. The pursuit of freedom requires an investment in this infrastructure, be it approval and payment of taxes, participation and care in the selection of those who will perform the services, or the exercise of self-discipline in observing the civil laws.

Nonetheless, the more that "procedures" conducted by civic employees take over, the less the time required for citizen engagement in civic duties, leaving more time for individual pursuits. One becomes less encumbered, more superficially involved with neighbors, less driven by a sense of civic duty and responsibility. There is little need to cultivate the democratic moral arts. The valued contingencies become those that sustain one's "rights" and way of life, not those most likely to sustain the good society. These are the contingencies that tend to keep people apart, that discourage the horizontal human connections communities require. Social capital is depleted.

The sustenance and renewal of socially democratic communities requires the existence or creation of a considerable amount of social capital in their citizens. James Coleman has presented us with a fascinating picture of decline in social capital in the transition of the United States from a highly agrarian to a predominantly urban, corporate, global economic power.[23] This change from one way of earning a living to another has been accompanied by a profound shift in virtually every aspect of life—from an ethos of horizontal to one of vertical relationships, from social capital invested in and derived from family and neighbor to financial capital independent of "family," from education in personal and civic virtue to schooling (and its credentials) as economic instrument. In sum, this transition has been accompanied by the loss of some moral center against which to check the validity of one's independent trajectory. And, too frequently, by the substitution of "my right to liberty" as the guiding criterion.

From the perspective of the democratic community, at least four unfortunate correlates accompanied the shift from social to financial capital described by Coleman. First, there was a strong decline in the *practical* knowledge capital that is essential to the infrastructure of a democratic community (that rejects servitude on principle). Second, this decline was accompanied by a devaluing of the experience from which practical knowledge, in contrast to academic or technical knowledge, is derived.[24] Third, bureaucratized procedures increasingly took over most aspects of community life, largely eliminating the process of citizens coming together to solve their problems. The town hall meeting and the conversation that went with it became an anachronism in a procedural republic.[25] Fourth, the slowing extension of the tools and benefits of democracy to those most disadvantaged and vulnerable in the pursuit of financial capital has narrowed the reach of *unum* by excluding an essential part of the *e pluribus* in *e pluribus unum*. A significant portion of the nation's political leadership appears to be oblivious to or unconcerned about these developments and the urgent need to shore up our democratic way of life on all fronts.

Increasing Educational Capital

With an increasing shift from the school as agent for the development of character[26] to school as economic instrument, the correlation between both the expectation for the possession of financial capital and becoming much-schooled also increased. With access to work most likely to ensure affluence requiring advanced schooling, part of the machinery for creating vast space between the haves and the have-nots was put in place. Today, far more young

African American men are in jail than in college. The rhetoric of "better schools mean better jobs" became a monstrous deception, suggesting that school reform rather than economic reform would affirm the American Dream. Those driving and supporting this rhetoric were well aware that the "best" schools would go to the most affluent and most-schooled parents, especially if they could get their hands into the public purse to help support their (private) schools of choice. The most insidious aspect of this deception was the implication that such would advantage the vulnerable and economically disadvantaged by enabling them, too, to attend these "best" schools.

The liberal movement in the United States of America, directed to equity in all realms of human endeavor, stumbled over the inflammatory issue of the distribution of wealth. At the time of writing, the malaise of the Democratic Party can be attributed to stepping delicately around this sword for fear of falling on it. Meanwhile, the Republican Party appears to be profiting from separating itself decisively from such notions as that of Richard Nixon at the beginning of his presidency regarding an assured minimum income for all.

Alexis de Toqueville noted many years ago our dedication to and admiration of the pursuit and attainment of affluence. Our image abroad is in large part one of devotion to such. Becoming rich is so built into the American psyche that even some of the most improbable aspirants turn their backs on notions of more equitable means of economic distribution for fear of having their own prospects flattened. Proposals regarding more equitable access to possible routes to financial capital are far more tolerable than are proposals that smack of more equitable policies and practices of distribution. The former connote the long term, whereas the latter could be enacted quickly. Consequently, concepts of universal education (couched as they are in benign language of the common good) do not raise the hackles to the degree stimulated by such proposals as severely progressive income tax structures.

Given this observation—and there is strong evidence for it—why not capitalize on it to gain the social capital our democracy needs to sustain family, school, community, and the nation? In the postmodern world referred to so frequently today, it is difficult to distinguish between social capital and educational capital so long as we keep our attention focused on education and self-transcendence and the relationships between the two as I have defined them on preceding pages. We begin to lose this focus on schools as the sole or even major developers of educational capital in today's society. This is not to deny either their public purpose or their potential educative power. It is simply to recognize that both this purpose and power have been corrupted by the intrusion of private purpose. Neither the public purpose nor the educative power of schools will be in good health until the educational capital of the surrounding context is raised significantly.

To put it more bluntly, I am saying that the notion of school reform as a tide raising the level of all boats is today both wrong-headed and mischievous. Wrong-headed because, as Thomas Green has insightfully observed,[27] even reform intended to help the disadvantaged helps the advantaged first. Mischievous because the dominance of private purpose in politically driven school reform of the past decade or so is not even directed to the impoverished and most needful. In effect, the concept that gave birth to and sustained a public system of schooling to ensure for all access to the knowledge and skills required for parenthood, work, citizenship, and personal comfort has been seriously eroded. Many people today, in contrast to those citizens who once connected such a system with both their own and the common good, are now devoted to the private cause of how to control and manipulate it for their own ends solely.

This group carries with it the sometimes unwitting support of the many more for whom the so-called underclass carries a host of negative connotations such as "street criminals, addicts, hustlers, alcoholics, drifters, the homeless, the mentally ill, welfare recipients, school dropouts, delinquents, residents of 'the projects,' illegal immigrants, teen-age gang members."[28] A popular view is that they would find jobs if they wanted work, ignoring the fact that the jobless now outnumber job vacancies by a ratio of at least six to one—and the further fact that schools do not create jobs. Scapegoating the poor is carried over into scapegoating the schools for what they cannot do, either.

Herbert Gans hypothesizes that scapegoating the poor postpones fundamental economic reform to which I referred earlier: a financial safty net (once proclaimed by President Ronald Reagan to be secure) and greater equity in the distribution of wealth (the Achilles' heel of liberalism). Gans proposes the familiar educational answer, with a quite unfamiliar caveat: "Education is still held out as the best escape from poverty, but only if the class structure is *not* reproduced, so that poor children get the best schools, teachers and equivalents for the preschool preparation more affluent parents can give their children."[29] The not-too-cynical critic might well respond: Pigs might fly but they are unlikely birds.

The "only if" that Gans prescribes for schools will not come without a profound shift in our associational attitudes that derive from education—the very education on which politically driven school reform is largely silent. The school is too much watched by those seeking its private use and too little watched by those most in need of the benefits of the public purpose and most lacking in the power to revive it. Consequently, we must look beyond the schools for the necessary educative contingencies. This does not remove the urgency of schools to contribute significantly to our educational capital. It is simply to say that their necessary renewal will not come quickly and will not, alone, be sufficient. Where, then, do we turn?

There are, I believe, two promising directions. The first, to be addressed later in this chapter, is to take advantage of present and potential opportunities for creating and expanding educational arenas lying beyond the scope of the coupled continuum of schooling that encompasses most children and youths from the age of 5 to the age of 18 and a sizeable percentage beyond. Many sound proposals are on the books for the education of the very young and "the forgotten half" between the ages of 16 and 24 not in school or college or planning to be; some of these proposals are in operation. These and others need to become universal. The second is to exploit consciously and deliberately the ubiquitous character of education by concentrating on how to transform nonlearning dependency on human services into learning experiences that strengthen the self. This translates into an enormous expansion of the informal and nonformal teaching force. The degree to which paraprofessionals and nonprofessionals in the health fields and, indeed, a growing number of physicians have helped us take responsibility for our own health through nutrition and exercise is a stunning example.

A critical part of this second approach involves sustained attention to the direction and nature of that "cacophony of teaching"[30] now occupying what Benjamin Barber refers to as civic space. Many of those persons involved in television production, for example, reject the idea that they educate or have any responsibility for such. The guiding criterion is the size of the viewing audience, not the cultivation of wisdom. Similarly, we must pay more attention to the purpose and meaning of human service when we are caught up in its systemics. Barber's anecdote is instructive:

People occupy civic space all the time; the trouble is, they seem not to know it. Not long ago, following a lecture on citizenship and civil society, a chastised middle-aged woman raised her hand and said to the speaker, "You shame me sir! Clearly, being a citizen is vitally important, but I have to tell you, what with my chairing the church bazaar committee, my service at the hospital, my assignment on the PTA, and my election to head my block association, I just don't have time to be a citizen![31]

One might conclude that this woman, like Alice discovering that she had been speaking prose all her life, would be pleased to be told that she is not only a citizen but a good one. But is she? In an earlier quote, Donna Kerr reminds us that the supreme test of a democratic society is "how we are with one another." To what extent does this woman contribute to development of the moral arts through these associations? In what ways does she advance the public purposes for sustaining the organizations of which she is a part? Organizations created to help educational and other human service agencies function must themselves become educative.

Transforming Human Service Agencies

Assuming that people are, indeed, the wealth of nations and, therefore, that the education necessary to the full development of individuals must be extended to all, then the ubiquitous nature of education must be exploited to the full. In other words, the boundaries that confine educational opportunities must be as few and as porous as possible so that access is democratized. Contrary rhetoric notwithstanding, this has never been the case with our schools. The recent stress on the specification and attainment of outcomes within the formal boundaries of schooling without accompanying attention to equity in inputs and educational conditions has worked against the democratization of access to knowledge.[32] The case for the public purpose of schooling in increasing educational capital for all has been overwhelmed by the surge toward the private purpose.

As might be expected, growing liberal alarm has brought forth strong counterarguments regarding the school's role in advancing democracy and a resurgence of interest in the ideas of John Dewey.[33] Dewey addressed the pivotal role of a truly common school but, as Robert Westbrook points out, he envisioned an ethical ideal of communities ensuring the necessary opportunities for every individual to realize his or her potential.[34] He spoke out not only against schools serving as tools for advancing the education of some at the expense of others but also against arrangements designed to bar for some participation in political, social, and cultural life.[35] "To extend the range and the fullness of sharing in the intellectual and spiritual resources of the community is the very meaning of community."[36] For Dewey, then, schools were simply a part of the total educative ecology.

The significance of ecological theory to this discussion resides in the degree to which the health of both the parts and the whole are interdependent. As with diseased organs in a human body, a sick entity in an ecosystem endangers the whole. But attention to such an entity as if it were detached from this whole will not suffice. Similarly, seeking to address the wellness of the whole without paying specific attention to malfunctioning parts will not be productive either.

As we shall see in Chapter 4, many of the regularities of schools reflect quite undemocratic beliefs and practices that not only exist in the surrounding culture but are massaged by contingencies deliberately sustained and promoted by this culture. Although schools should and often do struggle to mitigate the intrusion of these into their own beliefs and practices, their efforts are debilitating. Healthy cultures have healthy schools. Schools that contribute significantly to the education of the people are sustained by educative communities—communities in which growing up is accompanied by cultivation in the democratic moral arts. Such must not be left to schools alone. Nor is their potential to be ignored. Multiple educative possibilities must be mobilized.

Dewey stood strongly for action guided by the best use of intelligence—a democratic concept that tends to get lost in the clamor for representation. Action growing out of the ongoing conversation about democracy tends to be aborted by the stalemate over reconciling individual freedom and the common good within a conception of liberty. It has proved difficult to satisfy the thirst for freedom while arguing the case for protective restraints and to ensure common liberty while arguing the case for individual freedom. After addressing individual habits of the heart required for commitment in American democratic life, Robert Bellah and his colleagues were drawn to a consideration of the good society in which the individual moral arts might flourish.[37] The current danger to action lies in the tendency to separate rather than productively join the individual and the community moral arts. How we feel about and interact with one another in the symbiotics of family, friendship, and colleague-ship are not of a different genre from how we organize and conduct the symbiotics of larger associations. For one individual or one faction to gain power over another is not what should be sought in either. The need is to ground all associations in the same principles—principles enunciated earlier on which both secular and ecclesiastic theorists appear to agree.

Currently, as more and more people become concerned about an apparent decline in associational practice of the moral arts and in their own sense of community, there is a nostalgic looking back to a time when home, school, and religious institution sustained a relatively common set of values. If we just restate and promulgate these, many of us like to believe, the functioning, romanticized community we once had will be restored. "We must give our children . . . unequivocal, reliable standards of right and wrong," writes William Bennett in his introduction to their later explication: self-discipline, compassion, responsibility, friendship, work, perseverance, honesty, loyalty, and faith.[38] In going beyond the vague appeal to family values, Bennett at least helps to create a climate of awareness. But the image aroused by those who seek to define a moral compass is of an established infrastructure off course rather than on the rocks. In a culture of increasingly dysfunctional families, escalating rise in the voice of punishment and use of prisons for correction, and sharp parental scrutiny of schools seeking to go beyond the basics of rote learning, where and how are the desired dispositions to be learned?

Colin Greer and Herbert Kohl, addressing the same need, move us toward the necessary pedagogy in stressing the importance of strengthening children's beliefs through discussions around the themes of carefully selected books.[39] Walter Parker carries us further into understanding the need for and the disciplined routes to what he calls "the democratic mind." In a unique collection of essays from Dewey to contemporary thinkers, a changing tapestry of the 20th-century American experiment in democracy unfolds.[40] The public, civic purpose of education requires much more of method and scope than instruction in virtue by home and school. Our view of the citizenship now required must embrace not only an educational system that transcends and goes far beyond homes and schools but also teaching as the responsibility of all citizens. Each must think of herself or himself as part of a comprehensive educational delivery system instead of merely a client or user.

What does this mean? I have written elsewhere about the educative role of agencies and institutions beyond the schools.[41] The concept is one of each component of civic life, from day-care centers and nursery schools, to health and human service agencies, to the media, to businesses and corporations being self-consciously educative in civicness: the taking care of self and others in the entire range of community symbiotics. It means democratization of the Greek notion of the culture educating (*paideia*) expanded to include all citizens, not some. There is to be no underclass.

The concept itself is multidimensional. First, it is attitudinal. The physician is not there to relieve us of the responsibility to take care of our health. Each preventive or curative doctor-patient relationship is also a teacher-student relationship and, in many instances, a teacher-teacher association. The media know not censorship; they take responsibility for good choices (productive of educational capital) over bad (the promulgation of what is crass and vulgar). Business does not lambaste the schools for not specifically preparing its particular brand of workers. It adds specifically to what schools must do generally. There are no government agencies charged with monitoring agency or corporate acts of conscience or lack of it. But there are public expectations for civic conduct to be met—a public conscience that will require generations of democratic sensitization. The democratic mind does not come on full-blown.

Second, there is an interprofessional infrastructure that provides a common denominator for both community collaboration and civic education.[42] This denominator includes common attention not only to the educative role of each professional agency in civic space but also to the commitment and exercise of responsibility on the part of other entities. All professions include in their preparation programs some attention to moral and ethical behavior, a large part of which is subsequently lost or ignored in practice. There are common denominators in this lexicon. I envision a time when professional development centers, shared commonly by the health and human service agencies, will include in their in-service education programs attention to the democratic moral arts that should characterize their work and their educative role in civic life. The relevance of these to an aristocracy of everyone is nowhere more apparent than in the rhetoric of professional workers who address the needs of those who are most vulnerable in our society.[43]

Third, growing into responsible citizenship includes the acquisition of a pedagogy of caring and of sharing one's vocational and avocational expertise. A full life of parenting, friendship, work, and communal association involves teaching, for which most of us are ill-prepared. From early childhood on, the context of our learning should be one of learning twice—once for ourselves and once for the teaching roles in which we do and should find ourselves. Most of what is deliberately intended for our learning eschews the conditions necessary to learning, particularly those of active engagement involving conversation and hands-on engagement. John Dewey stated an important principle this way: "It is possible for the mind to develop interest in a routine or mechanical procedure if conditions are continually supplied which demand that mode of operation and preclude any other sort."[44] Six decades later, Jerome Bruner challenged both the creativity and the credulity of educators with a statement that became one of the most-quoted for years: "Any subject can be taught effectively to any child at any stage of development."[45]

John Carroll integrated a great deal of research into a model of classroom learning that emphasizes the design of opportunity[46]—a model that departs radically from the notions of "stuffing stuff" into the minds of children that have characterized conventional wisdom and, sadly, much of conventional practice. From the teaching of the young to the supervising of adults at work, the latter paradigm has been laced with rewards and punishments and embellished by a rhetoric of preaching, negative reinforcement, and rules to be enforced. This is not a pedagogy that incubates the moral community arts. Nor is it one that encourages each individual to diligently mentor others in expertise already acquired. The transfer of social capital is thus aborted.

A fourth dimension of a comprehensively conceived educational delivery system is the nature of its formalization. The educative attitude referred to above combines with the common denominators of professional engagement and the pedagogical principles that should characterize the everyday teaching encountered in growing up to condition the ubiquitous flow of education within and around civic space. They nurture and are nurtured by education's disregard of boundaries. Fully developed, these educational dimensions would obviate the need for more formal provisions. But fully developed they are not and never will be. The making of a just and caring society always will be a work in progress. An essential element is the making and observing of laws. The unpredictable deviousness of a portion of the population—a malaise to which no group is immune—requires such. Furthermore, this work in progress is one of renewal. Education is the most powerful renewing nutrient known to humankind.

Reliance on the pervasive, ubiquitous character of education is auspicious when a society already has in place contingencies cultivating all three of Oakeshott's idioms of moral condition: the morality of individuality, of community ties, and of the common good (Chapter 2). The flood of literary self-criticism in recent years tells us that such is far from the case in the United States of America, even though many people here and abroad share a vision of the possibilities. One reality is becoming increasingly apparent: Schools alone will not carry us to a realization of the vision, even though much of the blame heaped upon them is misplaced. We need a much more comprehensive system of education that includes redesigned schools (Chapter 4) and much more, with the whole directed toward the shaping of a civil society.

Toward a Comprehensive Educational Ecosystem

Thomas La Belle has argued the case for the integration of three overlapping learning systems in the community: formal, nonformal, and informal.[47] The formal is most clearly represented by the school system; the nonformal by beyond-the-school programs of instruction directed toward specific populations and their interests; the informal by that array of daily exposures to the environment, newspapers, television, friendships, and more. Running through all three today, with its future course and effects not yet charted, is the loosely harnessed, computer-based world of potential learning.[48]

The educational literature is rich in descriptions and analyses of the formal and nonformal; less so in regard to the informal. But the connections that might make a continuum of some of the parts or a system of the whole are largely missing. Instead, we have some excellent visions of a piece or pieces that, presumably, are to be joined to other pieces not addressed. The resulting dissonance reveals a fact of significant educational change: If a part of what now exists is redesigned or a new part added, whatever else exists must change or the new will not adhere to the whole and will perish. What was there before will remain and probably harden in its present configuration.

Consequently, we have a vista of educational reform littered with the carcasses of sometimes elegantly designed pieces that consumed their power before reaching their intended destination. One is reminded of the abandoned tanks and other military vehicles lying beside the roads of Israel that failed in their quest to reach Jerusalem. Seeking here to improve upon the descriptions of these pieces is neither desirable nor possible. Some of them are products of the long-term work of thoughtful individuals. Others are the results of commissions, often supported by philanthropic foundations, composed of able specialists and policymakers. The careful selection and joining of just a few, each addressing a phase of self-transcendence along the way toward maturity, begins to provide a vision of what could be—and, indeed, must be if our extensive rhetoric about kinder and gentler, caring for one another, and a civil society is to be more than empty of implementation.

Parental and Early Childhood Support Systems

Some readers will have noted that I am not attracted to the notion that new is best with respect to inquiry and ideas. The references I have drawn upon stretch across centuries, my memory across decades. In the decades since the 1972 report, *Early Childhood Education,* was prepared by the Task Force on Early Childhood Education (appointed by then California Superintendent of Public Instruction Wilson Riles), I have encountered no more succinctly comprehensive statement on needed parental and childhood support systems.[49]

Unlike many policy-directed documents, its first "statement of philosophy" addresses directly the need for a long-range commitment of public funds. Too many reports end with the sober conclusion that their recommendations will (probably) cost more and the impression (unintended) that the needed funds will not be forthcoming. The second statement leaves no ambiguity regarding the need to include all children, with the essential provisions for equitable access, a condition to be achieved through a close, collaborative liaison among educational, social, and health services. The participation of parents in all child-directed community activities is stressed, as is the need for education in parenting, not just in the prenatal period but during the adolescent years. Then, parents and children are to be enveloped in a safety net that brings together for their education and well-being the professions with their common denominators to which I referred earlier.

The language describing educational purposes and processes appears to have come from some much earlier era—perhaps that of Pestalozzi or Montessori. School is to be a happy place, with each child valued and recognized as unique (requiring, says the report, reduction in class size and elimination of large-group instruction).

Similar language can be found today in the writings of such individuals as Donna Kerr[50] and Nel Noddings,[51] and in Jane Roland Martin's conception of the schoolhome (built in part on the ideas of Maria Montessori and Johann Heinrich Pestalozzi).[52] But such language is almost entirely absent in the 1990s' rhetoric of discipline, standards, and world-class schools. Perhaps this is why so many teachers are cool to and not inspired by political calls to educational arms that so miss the inner core of seeking to connect significantly with children, the almost spiritual thing that brings them back each day in spite of the dispiriting circumstances around them and their work.

Early Childhood Education is much more than a synthesis of the ideas brought by able people to the conference table. Most members of the task force wrote drafts, drawing upon the most relevant research and on programs elsewhere such as the rich British experiences of the time with infant schools. After discussion and subsequent revision, these drafts were incorporated into the whole. I stress these procedures because so many of the plethora of school reform reports, for example, of the concluding decades of the 20th century ignored them, depending almost solely on the research and ideas generated by committees and their staffs.

Perhaps the most significant contribution of the California Task Force on Early Childhood Education was its concentration on the integration of the entire range of elements to be brought to bear on child rearing—a direction insightfully put forward by Superintendent Riles in his charge to the group. The services and nonformal education of the earliest years were to merge seamlessly with a school to be available to *all* children at the age of 4—to be available, not required. Then, the first 3 years were to be converted into a nongraded primary characterized by diagnostic evaluation and individualized instruction. "Nongrading" and "individualized instruction" may have been buzzwords of the time, but the concepts involved are reincarnated, with supporting research, in virtually every era of school reform, once attention to restructuring the public system of schooling comes down to focus on instructional circumstances.[53]

Given the degree to which we equate education and schooling and employ the words interchangeably, one would have expected an initiative put forward by the state superintendent of schools to concentrate on schools. But schools are addressed as only one part of an ecosystem of interacting physical, social, and psychological services, all sharing the common denominator of education with the schools. Among the recommendations specifically directed to schools, I regard as most significant the proposal to make access available at the age of 4.

Schooling

The decade from approximately 1985 to about 1995 may prove to be in our history the years of the most precipitous decline in the public association of the school and the American Dream and, indeed, of faith in both. The prospect is replete with ironies, most of them arising from misplaced expectations and myopic conceptions of cause and effect. That school reform failed is quite obvious. Whether and where the schools may have failed is not nearly as decipherable.

There is, so far as I am aware, no one report or combination of reports on schools and their improvement that comprehensively and simultaneously addresses both education in these institutions and their connection to the larger educational milieu of which they should be a connected part. This probably is because school reform reports are on schools, a subject so vast, complex, and intriguing that one becomes too engrossed in and ultimately exhausted by it to venture beyond. This I found to be the case with my own efforts to describe and analyze the place called school, reaching the 400-page anticipated limit of readers' patience in my treatise long before fully mining the databank put together by colleagues and me from only our own data.[54] Criticisms regarding my failure to move out beyond the commonplaces of schooling itself to the conditioning circumstances of an imperfect democracy were on target.[55]

This societal context has provided the direction of my movement in recent years—almost to the point of becoming so enmeshed in entanglements of our fast-changing society that my long-standing romance with schools is endangered. The trouble with both sets of interests is that they are of themselves so complex and intriguing that it is difficult to focus on connections. Consequently, I have decided to devote a chapter (4) intended to concentrate almost solely on the school's role in forwarding the interplay of education and democracy. This means eschewing the temptation to address the many changes in all aspects of their functioning that would occur if schools were to become the responsive, renewing institutions their good health requires. I confine myself here to just two sets of observations.

First, if we are to continue a deliberate, formal, systematic process resembling a schooling enterprise, however redefined—as I think we must—the greatest chance of making it work derives from how well we position it in life's major developmental passages. It cannot work as a place where toddlers are separated from their parents each day and dumped into a crucible designed to shape them for the nation's humanpower needs. What was recommended by the California Task Force on Early Childhood Education comes close to the desired model. When military and workplace demands such as those of Israel exist, an attractive alternative is the nursery-school model that closely resembles Martin's schoolhome.[56] For situations of no parents or one parent needing employment, the kibbutzim-based Israeli model has much to offer.

Transition from a relatively nonformal educative environment of the early years to a school geared to the developmental needs of children, requiring some but not as much involvement of parents, makes a good deal of sense, however, not only for parental convenience but especially for added educational stimulation and opportunity in the child's life. The school fulfills a much-needed custodial function that should in every way be safe, caring, and educational. The childhood years beyond 4 lend themselves well to a thorough grounding in the personal, social, and intellectual dispositions designed to serve well the years to follow. But a mismatch, not unknown even in good schools, grows in intensity as girls and then boys enter pubescence and adolescence. My recommendation of a 4-4-4 plan of schooling made accessible on a child's 4th birthday and ending with the 15th year errs only, I think, in this shortened period of school still being extended too long. Nonetheless, the discussion of Chapter 4 assumes such a reconstruction of the schooling years, an arrangement that makes increasing sense as nonformal educational opportunities beyond the school are deliberately and increasingly expanded during the concluding 4-year phase.

My argument for reducing the upper end of something resembling schooling as we have known it (while offering access a year earlier than is now customary) stems from the observation that the changes needed to successfully embrace 17- and 18-year-olds are far too extensive for accommodation even within the most flexible of school environments. These inadequate role models for younger children need to spend most of their time with older adults. The literature is not lacking in proposals worth considering.

The second observation to be made here is that schooling for the 4 to 16 age group must not be regarded as the whole of the educational environment to be provided. On one hand, a cessation of attention to and provision for the total support system recommended by the California Task Force when school commences will prove to be disabling for many of the children deprived of this social capital. On the other hand, there are powerful educative forces out there in the environment that teach without much thought to consequences. Studies have shown that children who would be seriously disadvantaged in readiness for school without benefit of an early childhood safety net lose ground in school when they no longer have it. There is no known dose of social capital that, when generously provided early on and then discontinued, compensates for this later absence. Further, ground not gained in one phase of early life is not easily recovered in later years. Regarding that milieu of teaching "out there," the assumption that good schools will overcome all that dehumanizes is egregiously naive. The task of sensitizing the dispensers of messages that debase is not, as I have said, a matter for censorship but one of education in the moral arts.

Adolescence and Young Adulthood

There is plenty of evidence for the observation that our system of public schooling was created in large part in response to tension in the adult labor market. Early on, children with a few years of schooling were valued in the labor force of a family-based agrarian society. The seasonal character of the school year was adjusted to the seasonal character of the farm year. With an accelerating shift to an industrial economy, older children constituted a pool of potential cheap labor welcomed by employers but quickly recognized by adult workers as a threat to their employment and wages. The secondary school expanded rapidly during the scarce-job era of the 1930s and the Great Depression. There had to be some comprehensive custodial arrangement for millions of young people who were neither accommodated nor wanted in the job market. Their daily confinement could be justified on moral grounds: They would become educated.

Three problems, dimly or not at all seen, soon arose to complicate both the custodial and the educational functions. First, the school into which came more and more adolescents had been designed earlier to accommodate some 10% of the age group in anticipation of most of them going on into college. There was no sudden movement to redesign the curriculum for the many newcomers who were not highly motivated to graduate from secondary school let alone enter college. The work of progressive, vocational, and life adjustment education advocates addressed the poor fit between schools and clients,[57] but decades passed before the concept of a comprehensive high school became the (debated) norm.[58] Nonetheless, school has not been and is not the place of choice, accomplishment, and satisfaction even for a substantial portion of the 75% who stay to graduate, a figure that has remained quite constant for decades.

Second, this lack of fit has been exacerbated by accelerating diversity in the student body. The system of schooling that adjusted sluggishly to a growing student population that varied mostly in interest and readiness was dramatically challenged by the heterogeneity in religious, ethnic, and racial characteristics of the cohorts that followed. The result was dissonance for parents, ill-prepared teachers, and many of the established norms of schooling, and disjunctures between students and the instructional materials and methods they encountered. Large numbers dropped out, many contributing to that "forgotten half" of older adolescents and young adults for whom not just our systems of schooling and education are ill-prepared but for whom the societal context is ill-adapted. In what may well be the most penetrating and deeply researched inquiry yet conducted and published, Scott Miller describes the devastating potential loss in individual satisfying lives and in the present and future well-being of this nation.[59] Unfortunately, the stark realities he documents are ills that most of our present political and business leaders and a disturbingly large number of well-established citizens prefer to ignore. The speed of travel down the information highway leaves no time to see the malaise behind the bushes by the roadside and to ponder where we might be headed.

The third unforeseen circumstance has been the steady age drop in the onset of pubescence—a drop of nearly 2 years over a 60-year span. The implications of this physiological transition take on increased significance when added to them are the changing perturbations in the lives of young adolescents growing up in rapidly changing social and demographic circumstances. The out-of-school culture has grown in significance as the influence of home, religion, and school have waned. With the growth of this culture has come an industry of media and business catering to it that has disclaimed responsibility for education in favor of the bottom line of financial profit. If a sitcom titillates adolescents' sexual awakening or mocks the stodginess of parents and school-based learning, or both, so be it. No wonder, then, that athletes, "good-looking kids," and gang members are favored over "smart kids" in the popularity polls of both junior and senior high school students.

Most politicians and dismayed opinion leaders seem unable to see beyond forms of punishment—such as the denial of financial assistance to teenage mothers of illegitimate children and more prisons for adolescent and young adult delinquents—to the larger, stagnant social and economic context that incubates the pestilence perceived. It is this perception of pestilence that drives policy and action, not the educational and other steps of prevention and renewal that must be taken. We like schools the way we remember them and resist change, even as we blame them for all manner of real and imagined shortcomings. Even so modest a measure as creating a middle school with cohort groups a year or so younger than those in the conventional junior high school arouses impassioned resistance, even as we lambaste the latter for not fulfilling the rhetoric of promise that accompanied its creation. We romanticize the civil circumstances of yesterday and envision their miraculous second coming without the discomfort of personal sacrifice, other than the building of more prisons for transgressors, on one hand, and sports palaces for our heroes, on the other.

The principle to which we must respond is that children and young adolescents should never be far from the attention of caring adults, and older adolescents and young adults should be the near-constant associates of still older, caring adults. Just as it takes a whole village to raise a child, it takes everyone beyond the years of childhood to create a village worthy of raising all children. Functioning families and morally grounded schools constitute a powerful combination for enculturating the young, but the school must be positioned somewhat downward in the life cycle. Even then, however, the upper years of the restructured school must connect productively outward with the nonformal and informal teaching that exists beyond. The connections upward in the life cycle are not at all clear. They require the rethinking of present educational settings and the creation of new ones if the transition from adolescence to adulthood is to be smoothed and productive lives are to result.

The work of two philanthropic foundations—the Carnegie Corporation of New York and the William T. Grant Foundation—is seminal. The concluding report in a series sponsored by the former, *Great Transitions*,[60] provides direction to pivotal institutions and interventions particularly on behalf of young adolescents. The latter, in a final report aptly titled *The Forgotten Half*,[61] takes on the daunting challenge of older adolescents and young adults, aged 16 to 24, not enrolled in our formal system of secondary and higher education schools.

Unlike most reports directed to critical problems of the young, that of the Carnegie Council eschews focus on specific targets such as drugs and single institutions such as schools. It assumes from extant research that serious problem behaviors tend to cluster and reinforce one another and that such behaviors have common antecedents. Consequently, remediation and, ultimately, healthy development require a clustering of initiatives and institutions. Unlike in most reports, the necessary role of organizations and institutions is not to be just service to clients but also responsibilities "for educating and motivating young adolescents in the pursuit of healthy lifestyles, for fostering interpersonal and decision-making skills to help them choose alternatives to very risky behavior, and for providing them with reasons and tools to build constructive lives."[62]

The educative ecology embraced by what the Carnegie Council refers to as a generic approach to both diagnosis and intervention includes families, schools, health agencies, and the media in the core community collaboration as well as a supporting role of business, government, universities, and scientific and professional organizations. Again, unlike in many other reports, the Carnegie Council advances an educative, self-disciplining role for the media, instead of the usual attack on the violence and unrestrained sexuality so often criticized and the common absence of recommendations.

At the time of this writing, there has been an insufficient interim for determining the degree to which the excellent work of the Carnegie Council conducted over a period of 8 years will penetrate public policy and local initiatives supported at state and federal levels. With respect to the reports of the William T. Grant Foundation Commission on Work, Family and Community published in 1988, however, several years have elapsed. The foundation supported an office to spread word of the recommendations and joined with the Annie E. Casey Foundation and Lilly Endowment to print and distribute a document directed to interagency collaboration in connecting families to comprehensive services.[63]

The final report of the Grant Commission appeared at a time when the topic of young people "at risk" was finding its way to the national rhetorical agenda. The Education Commission of the States played a vital role in alerting the governors. New organizations were formed that continue to meet on the implications to their largely professional members of large numbers of children, youths, and young adults whose problems and needs challenge existing institutions and point to omissions and shortcomings in both the safety net of helping agencies and the educational infrastructure. Much of what is recommended by the Carnegie Council for young adolescents is recommended by the Grant Commission for the older group—with a major addition: job-oriented vocational education and training.

By 1990, there was growing awareness that something more than world-class schools were needed to create and support a renewing capacity in vital elements of the nation's character. A sense of loss of community and of community well-being was growing. There was a strengthening push for job training to equip for self-sufficiency large numbers of that out-of-school forgotten half. But there also was an accelerating drop in security of employment and an increasing sense of personal and family insecurity. The conditions for fear were outpacing those for hope. Not long after the Grant Commission reports and other embryonic initiatives addressed to the serious situation with respect to large numbers of older adolescents and young adults began raising the tide of consciousness, that tide started to ebb. The more recent, concluding report of the Carnegie Council, with its recommendations for young adolescents extended to join those of the Grant Commission for the older group, reminds us that we have before us carefully crafted blueprints of what we must do but not yet the will to build what they so thoughtfully and inspiringly depict.

The Education That Runs Through It

This nation is faced with three imperatives on which the school's ability to fulfill its educational mission depends but which go beyond schools in their implications for democracy, education, and community. The first is extensively discussed in this chapter and several others: the need to address education in its own right, as instrumental to democracy as democracy is instrumental to education but to no lesser end. The second is the urgent need to shore up all of our health and human service agencies, not only to the end of extending them to all but also to the end of righting the inequities in regard to the readiness of all children to participate in the educational process and the human conversation. The third imperative is that these agencies become self-consciously educative, adding to the school's essentially academic approach opportunities to acquire the practical, experiential knowledge on which the community infrastructure depends so heavily. This is the least addressed part of the educational ecology now required.

The proposal that all of our young people engage for an extended period of time in some kind of community service is neither new nor radical. Alongside of this one, and growing in its advocacy, is the proposal for apprenticeships in job training. But rarely are these posed as further educational insurance (beyond that provided by schools) that the democratic moral arts will be acquired and refined. The first of these two proposals has the popular advantage of being a way to get the young off the streets and out of trouble. The second commonly is viewed as compensatory for those who take to academic learning slowly or poorly; vocational education always has suffered considerably from this "second chance" and "second best" stigma. It is time to elevate a combination of the two proposals to a level of educational status and public support their good health requires. Given the degree to which schools are muzzled in their freedom and ability to teach how and what a robust democracy requires, the need for this additional insurance is urgent.

Two major but not insurmountable obstacles to these proposals are cost and the degree to which our formal educational system encompasses the years of childhood, adolescence, and early adulthood in a tightly interlocking series of academic entities. These years of schooling provide a kind of half-education in what each successive entity requires of the other and promise highly valued credentials that correlate poorly with the virtues and verities so needed in a democratic society. This educational system appears to forget all those in the 16 to 22 age bracket not encompassed by it, and it resists mightily the rise of alternatives likely to compete for public funds devoted to the forgotten half.

Resolution will require bold, creative measures. One answer to both problems is a radical restructuring of the N–12 system as proposed earlier on these pages. Essentially it involves a downward extension of voluntary access to early childhood schooling to the age of 4, just as it was extended downward to age 5 decades ago, and normal termination of secondary school by the age of 16. This restructured, 4-4-4 plan of schooling would embrace the 4 through 7 cohort in the first unit, the 8 through 11 in the second, and the 12 through 15 in the third. We should be encouraged in this proposal by the experience of the Swiss in emphasizing the educational importance of the early childhood years and earlier completion of secondary school.[64] Only the exploitation of adolescents in school for the athletic entertainment of adults would suffer—a bonus for both schooling and society. The money saved by shortening by one year what we now know as schooling would pay a good deal of the costs for a period of community service, teaching, and experiential learning described below.

The bulk of the interns in community service would be, then, in the 16 to 18 age bracket. But one can envision the participation of older citizens attracted first by serving in specific teaching roles and, of course, immigrants seeking naturalization. Some in each cohort would go on into extended residencies in various human service agencies and businesses, just as large numbers would enter colleges and universities. Older citizens presumably would take sabbatical leaves for experiences that had not been available to them in early adulthood. Some, refreshed by the experience, would change their careers. Social policy to ensure the opportunity to return to previous jobs and the continuation of health care and other benefits would be essential.

Each intern would become a participant in the local, state, or national infrastructure through planned, guided immersion in essential elements of it: the functioning of health and other human services (child care, aid to the disabled and elderly, etc.), the ecology of open space and human habitation, the ecology of human enterprise (e.g., good work for employees and profit for the company) and the preservation of natural resources, the structure and conduct of government, the formal organization of political life, technology and communication, domestic and global commerce, and more. Internships would be accompanied by reflective seminars led by persons regarded as very competent in their fields of endeavor. A nonlinear, nondidactic kind of instruction would connect hands-on experiences, relevant reading, and individual internalization of the whole through disciplined conversation. Interns, modestly paid, would add to, not replace, persons engaged full-time as employees in the infrastructure. However, their participation would, in many cases, make it unnecessary to replace workers on sabbatical leave enjoying internships in some other part of the infrastructure. The movement of interns through the system and their contribution to it would help to balance out some of the costs.

If the proposed internship-apprenticeship program inserted into the coupled continuum of formal schooling is to function effectively, many people who view their present work responsibility only as getting the job done must self-consciously become teachers. It calls for every segment of the community infrastructure to become part of a culture of deliberate teaching in an educative community. The risk-taking in regard to becoming a more public persona and the loss of privacy that good teaching requires promote evaluative introspection: What do I have to give and how shall I give it?

The pedagogical method of disciplined conversation leaves no place to hide (which in part explains why so many teachers in schools and universities stay with the safer, more private didactic mode of teaching). In teaching from one's repertoire of expertise, there is always the potential of re-examining one's own work critically and seeking to do it better. One becomes introspective as a lay teacher about that teaching and about one's contribution to others in the community. The element of the infrastructure of which each individual is a part reaps the benefits. Democracy in education and education in democracy come closer together.

The subtle part of government intervention in all of the above is to raise moral consciousness, not stifle it through bureaucratic rules. There already exist in most communities voluntary services that fill in many of the gaps in government delivery of human services. For example, at the time of writing, former President Jimmy Carter is active in the coming together of what he calls "people of faith" representing almost all religious denominations for purposes of assisting the young to be more self-conscious about and attentive to their health. Dramatic increases in longevity are not the product of medical science and practice alone; people are learning to take care of themselves. Indeed, segments of the public virtually led the medical field into greater attention to nutrition and diet in the American family. We must become similarly educationally self-conscious in all aspects of living.

In paying more attention to building social capital through the cultivation of educative communities, we may be less inclined to blame the schools for our malaise and to hold them responsible for the nation's well-being. We can then reasonably expect them to fulfill their unique educational mission. Healthy nations have healthy schools. Healthy schools and robust democracies go hand in hand.

CHAPTER 4

Education and Schooling

A prominent politician stated recently, "We need less education and more training." From my perspective, the statement is silly. Unfortunately, it reflects a common perspective. Presumably, he fell into the mode of equating education and schooling. Then he viewed what schools do as too disconnected from market need. After all, much of the criticism of schools during the 1980s and 1990s has focused on their limp role in fueling the dominance of the United States in the global economy.

In the memory of many persons, school was once a rite of passage in the march toward work and adulthood. Most schools were quite small, even at the secondary level. The teachers lived and were known in the community and taught in the local school long enough for older boys and girls to pass on a good deal of lore about them to their younger siblings. It wasn't much fun to be truant or expelled because there wasn't much to do "out there" or many others to do it with—the out-of-school romanticized adventures of Tom and Huck notwithstanding. School provided some of the basic essentials for an adult life, but dropping out before high school graduation was not a tragedy. Indeed, many who did so received the job orientation and attained the seniority that kept them employed during the Great Depression of the 1930s.

The immediate aftermath of World War II paved the way for a profound change in the highly personal, relatively noninstrumental rite of passage that had been "school." The returning veterans had experienced a world far removed from the communities where they had grown up. The GI Bill promised an education and a life beyond that matched the cosmopolitan expectations that war had hatched. The postwar period brought jobs, wages, families, goods to buy, mobility, and even higher expectations. School became not a rite of passage but a ticket to a still better life for the children.

82

The number and size of schools increased dramatically. In the mid-1950s, the Los Angeles Unified School District required space for 500 new students every Monday morning—enough for a new elementary school. The midwestern community next to the small one where my family and I lived at the time gained national recognition for its design and later construction of a 5,000-student secondary school. School became big business—buildings, books, clothing, athletics, bicycles, motorcycles, automobiles, buses. School superintendents in the cities had little time for educational matters; they delegated these. They became business managers and were pleased to call themselves school executives. Associate superintendents for curriculum and instruction told me that they often camouflaged their specialty in seeking superintendencies. Many board members, they said, preferred candidates with titles such as associate superintendent for business affairs.

Not surprisingly, university preparation programs for school administrators, including principals, stressed management and finance. The "things" of schooling often took precedence over the human element. A complaint that was to intensify came from parents turned off by a growing impersonality in the schooling enterprise—an impersonality increased by tight union regulations regarding teachers' after-school time devoted to such matters as parent conferences. Some secondary school orientation evenings for parents at the beginning of a school year created the perception that these were sufficient for parent-teacher interaction until the beginning of the next year. The matters preoccupying the time and attention of school boards, superintendents, administrative staffs, and principals increasingly became those of managing the financial and organizational systems of the district and the regularities of the schools. Within this context, the teachers were to manage and teach their classes. Within this context, the children were to attend to their lessons.

This impersonal, systematized concept became "school," at least in urban environments. The place of humans interacting in teaching and learning became a statistic of so many students and teachers—PS 28 in New York City, for example—in the lexicon of funding and administering. The accompanying view of education in school was homogenized into an image of students passively receiving and teachers giving learning. Nonetheless, the school that was dead at night became a hive of activity in the morning and then settled into a custodial role embellished with learning activities. There is nothing about school as a system or school as a place that automatically imbues it with education. Like democracy, the wise conduct of education requires cultivated imagination, a condition rarely associated with bureaucracies and bureaucratic thinking.

In retrospect, it appears that two very different genres of "school" had emerged by the mid-1950s. One, school as a system, reified as a public enterprise, an entity of immense proportions, became a force for private, political, and national ends—a kind of dispersed educational Pentagon. The other genre, one of human properties—teachers, children, and parents—carried out the educational business of the first in local community-based settings, many of them still conducted very much like cottage industries. Although homogenized in the language and image of the business-oriented first genre and very similar in their regularities of operation,[1] each setting took on a different character from the humans associated with it. And these humans determined the degree to which education entered into the custodial role provided by this second school genre.

The reified system of public schooling placed and places an enormous imprint on the individual schools of the second genre. Parents and teachers may not carry in their minds a clear differentiation of the two, but they are caught up in the dissonance of the interactions. Linda McNeil has insightfully documented the contradictions in the minds of teachers who must choose between the messages coming to them from "the system" and those arising from their professional preparation and daily context.[2] In our research, my colleagues and I found a sharp split between teachers' idealized beliefs about teaching and learning and what they perceived the system to expect of them.[3] The difference between parents' positive ratings of the local school and negative ratings of schooling generally is, I believe, wrongly interpreted as complacency. A more accurate interpretation may be that they are not comparing "my school" with others but my school with "schooling."

This dual reality and perception must be understood if we are to gain lessons from the repeated failure of politically driven school reform eras. Otherwise, we will continue to demand of loosely coupled local entities what appear to be rational expectations for a multibillion-dollar corporation. The inevitable result is failure, disappointment, and discredited schools.

From Schoolhouse to School System

The postwar expansion and bureaucratization of schooling was a fact of the 1950s but not the central issue. The conversation among critics and parents alike was ideological and educational—about the what and how of teaching. Progressive education was taking its lumps. In his later years, John Dewey rose to defend progressive educators and practices from which he might readily have disassociated himself. He saw an attack on one as an attack on all.[4] Revered by liberal educators and universally acknowledged for his long period of intellectual leadership, he had for decades stirred the wrath of conservative critics. The floodgates that had released virulent criticism throughout most of his career opened wide in the years just before and after his death in 1952 (in his 93rd year).[5]

The debate was not confined to intellectuals and philosophical principles. It carried over into practices in many local schools, particularly those of the affluent suburbs. Newly prosperous young parents hovered over their children's education and schools. For every parent worried about a child's progress in school—and most were, regardless of that child's performance—proposals for change running counter to what he or she perceived current practice to be offered promise. Rudolf Flesch's name carried credibility from its association with how to write clearly. His attack on whole word, "look-say" approaches to the teaching of reading overstated the case but resonated with many parents for whom his recommended "return" to phonetic methods appealed.[6] "Back to basics" has been a popular slogan whenever kicking the schools has been in high fashion.

Even though the discussions and debates of morning coffee klatches and evening bridge games often were fueled by polemics such as Flesch's, the conversation was healthy. It often brought parents and teachers together over issues that should involve both and speakers of various viewpoints to PTA meetings. The system of schooling had become larger and more depersonalized, but the dialogue in and around many schools often was very close to the educational matters schools are for.

What many educators were slow to realize was the degree to which the questions raised by parents and the lively discussions around the schoolhouse were driven increasingly by a rising tide of educational conservatism pushing against what was perceived to have existed before and still. A major jolt of awareness was the 1951 ouster of the widely respected Willard Goslin, the progressive school superintendent of Pasadena, California, then a showplace of modern pedagogy, by a coalition of parents opposed to school taxes and progressivism.[7] It was easy for superintendents across the country to pass off what had occurred as a lapse of foresight on Goslin's part, but, for most, caution was now justified.

The so-called Pasadena Affair provided tangible evidence that the attack on progressive education was not to be confined to intellectual arenas and that the school interests of ambitious parents were not to be regarded as a passing fancy. Quietly, in 1955, the Progressive Education Association closed its doors. The Council on Basic Education, founded by Arthur Bestor who saw the excesses of progressive education to be regressive, opened its doors in 1956.[8] The educational conversation and controversy over such matters as life adjustment education as contrasted with subject-centered curricula and pedagogy did not abate. But the dominant attention to the schoolhouse was soon to shift dramatically to the school system and its connection to national interests at home and abroad: growing unemployment, growing crime and poverty, war and peace.

The Reform Decade of 1957–1967

There was rarely in discussions about the schools in the mid-1950s a theme of utter despair with respect to the conditions of schooling. Indeed, the increasing number of visitors from abroad, particularly from European countries, to see firsthand the great American experiment in universal schooling suggested evidence that the system was the envy of the world. The schools had been and still were part and parcel of the dynamic growth of the country and the nation and would continue to be so.

This long-standing belief was shattered in the fall of 1957 when a small Soviet satellite was reported to be circling the earth, less than an hour's drive away if there were roads and automobiles proceeding straight up. Suddenly, the schools were perceived in a larger context. Out of the shock, there was an opportunity for introspection, for serious reflection and analysis of where the nation was headed, what it valued, and the relationship between education and a social and political democracy. The ongoing conversation over the schools was narrow and often self-serving. T. S. Eliot had spoken earlier to this larger context:

> If education today seems to deteriorate, if it seems to become more chaotic and meaningless, it is primarily because we have no settled and satisfactory arrangement of society, and because we have both vague and diverse opinions about the kind of society we want. Education is a subject which cannot be discussed in a void: our questions raise other questions, social, economic, financial, political. And the bearings are on more ultimate problems even than these: to know what

we want in education we must know what we want in general, we must derive our theory of education from our philosophy of life.[9]

The introspection and conversation implied by Eliot were not what ensued. The blame for apparent slippage in assumed U.S. technological superiority was laid on the schools. Their charge, political and business leaders proclaimed, was to establish this superiority unequivocally by ensuring that the Soviets would be beaten in the race to dominate in outer space. This is not the first time in the history of American schooling that the schools were used to draw attention away from those responsible for industrial, trade, and monetary policies. But it may have been one of the most crass. Nothing was said later in praise of the schools for subsequent U.S. achievements in technology and space. Of course, to have credited the schools would have been nice but foolish since so many of these achievements came years before the graduates of reformed schools could possibly have made any difference.

The rhetoric of politically driven school reform called for a toughening up of practices gone soft; more rigorous curricula in mathematics and science were to lead the way. Directives to school administrators, passed along and down to be acted upon by teachers, included techniques that came straight from business and military linear models of efficiency. Ironically, many of these were later abandoned by large segments of the business-corporate world, but they became well established in the litany and ways of the school system. Some of the popular procedures that came to dominate in-service training programs for teachers and guidelines for seeking federal research and development grants were presumed by advocates to be too rational to challenge: minutely defined objectives, planning done backward from clear goal definition, feedback loops, evaluation to assure no breaks in the linear chain, and the like. Raymond Callahan is cited again and again in educational literature for his prescient warnings of a cult of efficiency.[10] The assumptions of passivity and inability of teachers to effect innovation virtually assured slippage in the changes proposed.[11]

The heavy action of the reform era moved to Washington, D.C. The system of schooling responded as the rhetoric of criticism escalated to a point of overkill. School executives now had a more daunting and potentially more rewarding challenge than overseeing the construction of new buildings. They had a school reform movement of national consequences to direct and manage.

My purpose is not to present, one more time, a short review of a much-documented time in the history of American schooling. It is, rather, to note a momentous upsurge of federal use of the school system in the service of the nation—first to engage in a cold war with the U.S.S.R. and then as a pillar in President Lyndon Johnson's plans for the Great Society, peaking in the 1965 Elementary and Secondary Education Act (ESEA). Schooling took on the business and political trappings that go with the control and distribution of billions of dollars. The reification of education into a school system became sharply etched—and strengthened the embryonic view that the federal government should be out of it and, indeed, that the public schools should be abolished.

It was a fruitful time for educators, nonetheless. John Gardner, the architect of ESEA and soon to be secretary of the Department of Health, Education, and Welfare (HEW), was commanding officer of the White House Conference on Education of 1965 that addressed implications and implementation of the ESEA. Long associated with the educational philanthropy of the Carnegie Corporation of New York, he and his chief lieutenant, U.S. Commissioner of Education Francis Keppel, were viewed as strong advocates and friends of education and the schools. The key players they invited to Washington in the name of President Johnson were school board members, educational lay leaders, and educators from schools and universities. Invitees were charged with carrying out an educational revolution (that soon was to languish in the shadow of the Vietnam War and the interests of a new president for whom schooling was not a high priority).

Although the script of the 1957 to 1967 era of school reform resembled in many ways that of the era that was to emerge in the 1980s, the scenarios, in sharp contrast to those of the education summits that characterized the latter, featured actors whose life-long career commitments and engagements were in education. Acknowledging that they presumably had much yet to learn from business and political domains, it was assumed that they would carry out the needed reforms, nonetheless.

Even though the rhetoric of expectations for schools subsided in the late 1960s almost as quickly as it had risen in the late 1950s, the appropriations authorized in 1965 continued. There was funding to provide so-called compensatory education for the vulnerable and disadvantaged, unprecedented infusion of dollars into research and development, financial support to local collaborative projects, and more. There was accumulated in subsequent years a body of knowledge about learning, teaching, evaluation, and processes of change sufficient to have provided considerable guidance to the renaissance in schooling that was soon to be of little public interest and did not occur. Simultaneously, there was growing a perception that the school system had failed and neither should nor could be resuscitated by either educators or this knowledge. Indeed, both were seen as largely irrelevant by reformers outside the system. Their attacks gained support and legitimacy from the even harsher ones of critics initially inside the system who authenticated their criticisms with educational credentials even as they moved out of the system to what they perceived to be higher ground.

I view that decade as the first of two school reform eras in the second half of the 20th century that transformed for a large segment of the public its nostalgic image of school as the little red schoolhouse to one of a bureaucratic system attached to the political and business marketplace. The personalized symbol of a rite of passage in childhood was increasingly obscured by the emergence of an enterprise run by and for adults, to be fought over by adults in ways and for reasons beyond the comprehension of children. The fallout from this first era, hardened into place by the second, was the emergence of market values and principles over educational ones in both expectations for and management of the system of schooling, misnamed "the educational system." In the process, imbuing the system with educational concepts and principles—through its thousands of loosely coupled local entities constituting that second genre of schooling—became more difficult.

The Reform Decade of 1983–1993

The steam ran out of this school reform era in the closing years of the 1960s. Simultaneously, it seems, the effervescence of the educational conversation stimulated by both genres of school died down. The prolonged Vietnam War played a debilitating role. Scientists and astronauts had satellites of various kinds in outer space before "reformed" schools could possibly have produced their brilliant graduates to do the job. Academic accomplishments in mathematics and science were somewhat ahead of where they had been, accusations to the contrary notwithstanding, but not enough to create much joy. The 1970s settled into a period of lowered enthusiasm for both the American Dream and the schools. The plight of those at the margins of opportunity grew more serious and potentially explosive. The faith index of those in occupations once admired—doctors, lawyers, politicians—declined. School reform dropped significantly from public attention.

The federal funds for research and development in several major areas of human interest accelerated a momentous shift taking place in the emphases of higher education from the late 1950s into the late 1980s. Undergraduate teaching lost ground to funded research in the priorities of faculty members, particularly in flagship, doctoral degree–granting universities but significantly, also, in state universities that had once been teachers' colleges.[12] Schools and colleges of education in which the preparation of teachers had recently been the top priority endeavored, with mixed success, to emulate the scholarly emphases and research methods of the liberal arts, particularly the social sciences.[13] Formerly quite closely connected with the schools and state regulatory bodies in teacher credentialing, colleges of education pulled back, especially in the most prestigious public and private universities. Continued association with schools and their problems, particularly in urban settings, commonly was seen as detrimental to the status of these colleges on their own campuses and to the advancement of their professors. Of the top-ranked half-dozen schools of education in a 1977 report, several produced no teachers for the schools and only one produced a significant number.[14]

Although the decade of the 1970s was a period of relative calm with respect to schools, troubles soon to be blamed on schools still another time were brewing. Unlike the end of World War II, the end of the Vietnam War produced neither a national feeling of pride nor a surge of economic well-being. The economies of some other countries, particularly Germany and Japan, were flourishing. The problems of unemployment, crime and violence, health and general well-being of the poor, and urban decay that were to be taken care of by the Great Society, and particularly its reformed schools, were growing more severe. The entry of drugs into all walks of life increasingly became a compounding factor. Funds once directed to school change and innovation were being shifted to evaluation of federally financed programs and increasingly widespread standardized testing. The time and money spent on examining ongoing activities probably exceeded that spent on intended improvement.

The schools were blamed for our malaise—one more time. Instead of the Soviet *Sputnik* of 1957 serving as the catalyst, it was a commissioned report of 1983 stimulated in large part by the growing dominance of foreign-made goods in the consuming sector of the U.S. economy—automobiles, television sets, household appliances, and the tools and machines of our own domestic production. Thrown into this mix as a major causal factor was the poor performance of our schools, as evidenced by the low test scores—those of the early 1970s. (When *A Nation at Risk*[15] was released, scores had been on the rise for several years.)

This time, the schools were to be thrown at our declining competitive position in the global economy. Once again, there was to be a general toughening up of schools gone soft: a longer school week and year, more basic subjects and courses in the curriculum, a greater emphasis on mathematics and the sciences. Since teachers were at fault, increases in their salaries were to come only if student performance improved; merit pay would follow meritorious results. But the militarylike call to arms offered no new weaponry to educators.

More crassly than before, the political instrumentality of school reform was grasped by governors and legislatures. The rhetoric was much less directed than before to the social fabric of the nation and much more to its economy and to the individual pocketbook. This time, the federal role was much more self-protective and adroit, more cheerleading than leading. The action was to be at state and local levels. The federal role was, in part, to paint the bleak picture, set broad goals, stay clear of maps and blueprints, remain in the wings, and then step forward from time to time to proclaim progress and need and, ultimately, success.

President George Bush's secretary of education, Lamar Alexander, took to this role as though born into it. Regular newsletters emanating from his department proclaimed the lofty goals of America 2000 —from having all children ready for school to world leadership in mathematics and science—to be attained by the year 2000. The train was leaving the station; whole cities were ticketed to get on board when their mayors signed up for the trip. The routes were not specified; presumably these and other details would be discussed after embarkation. Unlike the reform era of 1957 to 1967, the period of the Reagan–Bush presidencies brought forward no major funding initiatives. Indeed, there was a virtually unprecedented appeal to the private sector. Most of the corporations invited to join in backed off. Many now had their own philanthropic initiatives in school reform under way. Some of these became almost the only ones supporting agendas later identified as being forwarded with some success.

Although the driving forces of the earlier era had a rather dim view of the capabilities of educators, there was the expectation that they could learn and do what was required of them. Many of the bright young scholars brought into the National Institute of Education in Washington, for example, who assumed responsibility for the disbursement of federal funds, often scornful behind the scenes of those seeking grants, nonetheless assumed that they could shape the process so that recipients could achieve results. Over time, bonds were formed that produced some mutual respect and some fruitful learning on both sides. Professors of education were brought into key positions in the Department of Health, Education, and Welfare; social scientists from federal offices frequently left to assume professorial roles in research-oriented schools of education.

Nothing paralleling this occurred in the later era. Although prominent educators were brought into significant leadership roles in the federal government and used their educational credentials when convenient to do so, the dim views of several of the most outspoken regarding "the education establishment" strained relationships with former colleagues who were now exhorted to get on the reform train. Few did. Universities came under increasing criticism from political and business sectors for their aloofness from the reform movement.

There was some justification for the criticism. I already have referred to the degree to which schools of education withdrew from involvement in elementary and secondary schools and then, notably in the major universities, from teacher education. Increasingly, the rewards were for research and publication. Furthermore, the dominant quantitative research methods, focused on individuals as the units of selection, did not lend themselves to studies of whole schools and complex processes of change. The more promising qualitative methods such as case studies were slowly gaining use and more slowly gaining approval in the faculty reward system.

Nonetheless, on the campuses of virtually all large universities, predominantly in the more heavily populated areas, hundreds of faculty members representing professional schools and the arts and sciences were getting involved in schools and communities, mostly those from which they received the bulk of their student bodies. Some of these initiatives involved an individual or clutch of individuals from a professional school such as public health or architecture and urban planning working with collaborators in the community; many brought professors in the arts and sciences into schools to work with teachers on curriculum improvement projects; several brought universities and school districts into formal and informal partnerships to address an array of mutual interests.[16]

Private philanthropists, corporate foundations, and such federal agencies as the National Science Foundation, the National Endowment for the Humanities, and the National Endowment for the Arts were sources of funding. Apathetic perhaps to a call to arms couched in the rhetoric of U.S. competition in the world economy and better schools for better jobs, university personnel frequently worked beyond their campuses in matters that connected with their scholarly interests. To say, however, that universities did not join wholeheartedly in the politically driven exhortation to make the schools a powerful instrument in the nation's economy is a fair assessment.

Another fair assessment is that school-based educators—teachers and principals—did not rise enthusiastically to the call for the nation to ride triumphantly into worldwide economic superiority on the backs of their schools. When Secretary Alexander signed up an America 2000 city, teachers were busily conducting their classes as usual. The message to a city regarding the six national goals to be attained addressed the mayor, the city council, and business leaders but not always the superintendent of schools. In 1991 and 1992, several years into President Bush's call for "new schools for a new world," I asked about a dozen audiences ranging in size from about 200 to more than 1,000 teachers, administrators, professors, policymakers, and parents to respond to the question, "How many of you know the basics of America 2000 well enough to explain them to someone else?" The showing of hands ranged from 2 or 3 to a high of 14.[17] By April 1992, the *America 2000 Newsletter* had announced a veritable landslide of communities committed to the program. Clearly, the gap between this rhetoric and the awareness of the educators who were to achieve the goals was enormous.

The general absence of university professors and schoolteachers from the politically proclaimed revolution was explained by educational advisers to Bush and Alexander as symptomatic of the prevailing lethargy, much like that of parents giving high marks to their local schools: "They just don't get it." Or, could it have been that many were becoming increasingly aware of the silliness of the rhetoric and the emptiness of the strategy? To the degree that educators did board the train—and some did, as an act of conscience, because there were vague promises of money, or out of fear of appearing uncommitted and insensitive[18]—they became part of the problem, subsequently sharing with politicians responsibility for loss of public confidence in the school system.

There was a brief time in the late 1980s when it appeared that a grassroots theme gaining ground with local schools and a systemic theme of restructuring schooling gaining the attention of governors and state legislators were sufficiently close in concept to drive the renaissance that had not yet surfaced. Local lay leaders and educators spoke of the power of site-based management, a scheme of moving greater authority, with accompanying responsibility, for decisions to the principal, teachers, and parents of the school. Scholarly interest in the power of school culture and the school as the locus or center of change[19] was beginning to penetrate the conferences and in-service education programs of teachers and administrators. In part out of frustration with their top-down efforts to inject change into the system and in part out of belief in the idea, state policymakers began to push for "empowering" those at the individual school sites. Several philanthropic foundations already were expressing cautious enthusiasm for projects directing funds to school settings. University personnel now getting increasingly interested in studying school change and innovation discovered that successful requests for funds required evidence of collaboration with schools and school districts.

The opportunity faded more quickly than it had emerged. School as the nation's potential guiding light and savior had been grossly oversold. There was plenty of evidence by the early 1990s of schools in all regions of the United States, notably at the elementary level, that were more than holding their own in the face of changing family and community conditions that seriously impacted their work.[20] Some of these were tied variously to the ideas and initiatives of such highly visible leaders as James Comer, Howard Gardner, Henry Levin, and Theodore Sizer, this last named making progress at the secondary level with his Coalition of Essential Schools. Their work advanced ideas increasingly supported by research as sound: the need for home and school to work in close collaboration, the need for multiple approaches to ensure that all students learn, the need to involve students as workers in a coherent curriculum rather than as passive listeners to teachers who do all the talking, and more.[21] But the genre of the local schoolhouse as the essence of American schooling was not the one of attention. Chester Finn, frequent spokesman for the dominant political interest in the school system at the time, dismissed these efforts along with whatever others of promise were under way as a ho-hum revolution.[22] The message was that the executive branch in Washington, through its Department of Education, had blown the bugle and declared a crusade, but the educators had not responded.

America 2000 blew away on election day in November 1992. A much less trumpeted Goals 2000 became the Democratic resuscitation. President Clinton could not be expected to abandon the education goals he and other governors had put before President Bush at the Education Summit the latter convened shortly after his election. But the tide that had raised expectations for the schools was ebbing. There had been no celebration of school accomplishments during the final months of the Bush presidency. The much-heralded "standards" movement initiated on his watch was getting into troubled waters. Indeed, Lynn Cheney, who, as head of the National Endowment for the Humanities, had closely identified herself with its grant to develop higher standards for the teaching of history was soon to become a leading critic of the results—and of the National Endowment itself.

Cheney was not alone in turning on the office that had so recently nested her. Two secretaries of education of the Reagan and Bush administrations—William Bennett and Lamar Alexander—proposed abolition of their department early in the Clinton years. Lesser officials for whom their positions in the federal government had gained them recognition walked away with nothing good to say about the public schools or the reform initiatives with which they had been associated. Although some of what they had promoted continued, usually wrapped in different language, the new administration was turning in the wrong direction, they explained. A common theme of those departing was that the federal role in education should be downsized in favor of greater privatization; several stepped into lucrative roles designed with that in mind.

There should be some fitting punishment for those just out of office suddenly grown clairvoyant regarding what they would do if once more in. The punishment should be intensified for those now out who disclaim or denounce that for which they were only recently responsible.

There was not in 1993 a sudden stoppage in financial support—federal, state, and local—for the American school system. But the economy was probably the central issue in the elections of 1992 and the surprising come-from-behind presidential victory of Bill Clinton. Education had ranked quite high in his campaign rhetoric, but there was no 1993 launching of a new, comprehensive education bill or national commission on school reform. Other matters such as health care dominated the federal agenda. As stated earlier, there was growing citizen hostility to such matters as standards setting and, indeed, educational prescriptions coming from Washington. The school reform era that began in 1983 with devastating criticism of a school system viewed as central to the nation's well-being and that had been politically sustained beyond early expectations was over. There were not, to mark this now-apparent fact, any unusual perturbations in the system or in the many thousands of local schoolhouses.

Some Reflections and Lessons

Three results from politically driven eras that address school reform as instrumental to national social and economic well-being are predictable. First, little learning from earlier eras is carried into new ones, even when comprehensive postmortems are available. Indeed, such tend to be discredited as impediments to the fast-track progress anticipated and declared. Cautionary words are not welcomed and frequently are discredited as irrational or even unpatriotic. Was the silence of so many educators during the so-very-crass political era of the 1980s into the 1990s the result of not wishing to appear uncooperative? The obvious silliness of blaming our global economic woes on a decline in test scores places great demands on one's restraint[23]—too much, one would think, to hold back at least a few words of skepticism. In retrospect at least, one must express concern about a formal educational system that seemingly had failed over the years to develop in the people sufficient understanding of what education is for them to see its corruption in the political and business marketplace. The degree to which schools are subject to manipulation endangers their ability to educate.

Second, silly though it may be to address the school system as though it derives a kind of turbocharged power from myriad parts that completely lack any mechanical or technological connections, this holistic reification is incredibly damaging to the infrastructure and, eventually, the morale of a society. At best, such serves only the interests of a temporary régime or collective. The ultimate self-serving strategy is disassociation from claims once made and from failure. The insidiousness is in the claims made: Reformed schools will cure our malaise and satisfy our wants, however self-serving. One fallout of inevitable failure is loss of faith in the schools for not doing what they cannot and should not be asked to do, a sinking usually to a point below where they were said to be when the need for reform was proclaimed. The second fallout is failure to recognize or to address the myriad societal problems requiring early and direct attention. The schools experience a cycle of being blamed, scapegoated, burdened with unrealistic expectations, and then perceived to have failed. What rarely is noted is the failure of reform.

Third, by the time the nation's problems and issues requiring remedial action are properly diagnosed and addressed, the schools are regarded as irrelevant, ineffective, and not deserving of the attention and resources they need for what they can and should do. The failure of school reform and the failure of schools become one. Likewise, the impersonal, systematized concept of school embraces in its fall from grace the local schoolhouse, except for some of the parents closely associated with it—now less than a third of the adult population. And since the schoolhouse has been drafted into the system, so to speak, for the war against poverty, violence, crime, and unemployment at home (in the Great Society rhetoric of the 1960s), international competition in outer space (the 1960s), and global economic competition abroad (the 1980s), the local school is now expected to have increased personal payoff. After all, "better schools mean better jobs."[24] The public purpose of schooling is subverted in favor of the private one. It becomes more difficult for schools to serve their educational, democratic mission. Robert Westbrook sums up the consequences of the market-driven school system:

> On the whole, then, the twentieth century has witnessed the rapid rise to preeminence of schooling for . . . "occupational competence" and the relegation of civic education to, at best, an afterthought. Once the principal institution for vocational training, the high school has now become for many students a station on their way to enrollment in a new layer of "differentiated" schooling. . . . One is far more likely to hear one's child spoken of as "human capital" than as a citizen in waiting. American public schools have become, above all, a vast, variegated system funnelling this human capital into its final destination in the hierarchies of the undemocratic world of modern work.[25]

Indictment of misdirected school reform movements does not absolve the schools from their much-documented educational shortcomings. The time period surrounding publication of *A Nation at Risk*, addressed to the school system, was accompanied by publication of several inquiry-based books addressed to the schools. Three of these were in very close agreement regarding the schools' shortcomings: too much teacher talk to passive students, emphasis on the lower levels of cognition, unbalanced curricula, classification of students into self-fulfilling prophecies of success and failure, a cluttered school day at the high school level, loss of learning time to school and classroom routines, a low profile for academic excellence in the culture of the school, a mismatch between oft-articulated goals of schooling and testing, and much more (including the authors' varied perceptions of how the fundamental purposes of education were shortchanged).[26] Their criticisms of schools were widely cited in the hundreds of politically commissioned reports that appeared in succeeding months, adding to the picture of poorly functioning schools. Their many recommendations were largely ignored, the omission serving to make more conspicuous the near-absence of educational concepts and principles in the reform agendas of the succeeding decade.

This omission may help to explain the tepid response of educators that so infuriated some legislators and business leaders during the highly charged reform years of the 1980s. For all their differences, school and college teachers share a common commitment to a variously defined and conducted culture of teaching and learning commonly equated with education and schooling. Although twisted and often corrupted by the marketplace culture that seeks to bend it to economic purposes and principles, the culture of teaching and learning prevails in the daily lives of those who come each day to carry on their work in the schoolhouse, be it the local elementary school, college, or university. Their pace, their hearts, their minds simply do not quicken to the message, better schools mean better jobs. They respond to quite different drummers: the 8:30 a.m. algebra class to be taught, the challenges of controlling adolescent exuberance, racial tension in the hallways, children half-asleep, that child who most surely is dyslexic. Does it surprise you, Mr. Finn, that for most of them the crusade that failed to arouse them was a ho-hum revolution?

A fourth book of the time helps us to understand this culture of teaching and learning that must be reckoned with in the critically important business of helping schools become the educational settings they should be—and many people prefer them not to be. Sara Lawrence Lightfoot, in *The Good High School*, described six very different high schools in six different settings, with six different mixtures of students, all managing to take care of their business, and each at very different places on the testing continuum that measures success.[27] What each of these needed to do to improve was very different and could not be determined on any less information than the comprehensive portrait provided by Lightfoot after weeks of visiting each, observing, and talking with a great many people. Even then, she was cautious, taking great pains to sketch key components of the ecosystem of each school that would powerfully influence internally driven processes of renewal and reactions to any externally driven improvement intrusion.

The simplistic paradigms of change accompanying the reform eras described on preceding pages are consistent in their self-inflicted blindness to the culture of individual schools, particularly the politics of their daily functioning. Failure is their inevitable destiny. This blindness leads also to the misguided, face-saving conclusion, when the reality of failure no longer can be ignored, that it was the schools and not the reforms that failed, and that it was those in the schools and not the reformers who were naive. Such faulty diagnoses nourish the seeds of the next doomed era of reform.

From School System to Schoolhouse

The general failure of large-scale efforts to restructure the school system has led to cynicism and dissatisfaction on the part of many people—both those who sought to effect it and those who observed or were affected by the efforts. The former group attaches blame to intractable educators, not their own change strategies. The latter group attaches most of the blame to a bureaucratic system and decisions made too far from the schoolhouse. Both groups favor decentralization. Their proposals range from dismantling the system in favor of privatization to placing much more authority in the hands of local councils within a decentralized public system. The specifics range from some kind of contractual franchising, to charter schools, to vouchers for public or private schools of choice. Common to most proposals is the intent of getting spending close to the schoolhouse. Frequently, market principles of accountability, tied to performance incentives for teachers, are proposed.[28] Micropolitics are to replace macropolitics.

On the surface, this sea change in the politics of schooling appears to mesh with the recommendations of grassroots reformers and serious students of school change processes regarding the school as the center of improvement, referred to earlier in the chapter. But the resemblances turn out to be superficial. Most grassroots reformers and improvement-oriented students of change ground their efforts and proposals in educational reasons, reasons that range from comprehensive theories regarding the culture of schools and classrooms to narrower theories regarding how people learn and how teaching should proceed. Frequently, they present agendas based on educational principles.

By contrast, persons advocating dismantling or decentralizing the system tend to be preoccupied with shifts in the loci of power. They assume that "better" education for children and youths will result. Beyond advocacy of privatization, vouchers, schools of choice, charter schools, and so on—proposals that tend to become sloganized—they are short on educational purposes, concepts, and principles. These are details to be worked out later. In effect, there is faith and an expectation of similar faith on the part of others with whom the details presumably will be addressed. After all, isn't this what democracy is all about?

However, before the inquirer is ready to dismantle what we now have, he or she might desire to gain some understanding of what advocates have in mind to replace it. It would be helpful to have at least some opinions informed by reading, reflection, open forums, perhaps even debates. After all, isn't this what democracy is all about? Unfortunately, faith and reason often are at loggerheads. If faith is put forward when reasons are sought, inquiry is subverted. The inquirer may be branded an infidel. Faith and power join; conversation is subverted.

There is no question that the system genre of schooling against which politically driven reform movements such as those described on preceding pages are directed cries out for fundamental redesign. However, the expectation that replacing macropolitics with micropolitics will give us better schools—better, say, in serving the public as well as their private purpose—must rest on more than faith. We must have before us more than charges of inefficiency and personal preferences before we join a new crusade. After reviewing school reform from colonial days to the present, Timothy McMannon observes:

> A first step toward genuine school improvement . . . is to insist that reformers clarify their rhetoric. We, as potential participants in and judges of reform, must require innovations and their champions to adhere to a kind of truth-in-labeling law. What is really behind the suggestion? Is it actually intended to improve the educational experience of children in the schools or is there some non-educational efficiency motive driving it?[29]

Micropolitics and School Improvement

As one who views schooling as more a cottage industry than a big business, the individual school as the center of renewal, and micropolitics as potentially more satisfying than macropolitics, I would like to substitute opinion authorized by knowledge and experience for blind faith in advocating massive decentralization of our system of schooling. There is nothing in the nature of micropolitics, however, that ensures moral superiority over the nature of macropolitics. There are many places and circumstances in this nation where the values uppermost in the local power struggle lag far behind both the visions for and the principles of democracy. I find myself with respect to school improvement close to what I perceive the stance of Michael Fullan to be. After reflecting on his own years of inquiry and the work of others, he sees individual schools as key centers of change in the context of a larger support system driven by public moral purpose.[30]

I fear that one of the major expectations for the decentralization of schooling is enhancement of private purpose. The central issue in balancing authority and responsibility for our schools is how best to position them for advancing the mission of enculturating the young critically in a social and political democracy. The future of humankind depends heavily on whether we come to understand the meaning of liberty and learn to balance freedom with responsibility.

The difficulties inherent in empowering our schools for such a mission are neither removed nor fundamentally changed by radically shifting the loci of decision making. Some problems will fade, to be replaced by others. What will continue to be evident and troublesome stems directly from our chronic neglect of education: there has been an absence of conversation about what education is, what it has to do with democracy, and what this democracy's schools are for. Preparing for parenthood and citizenship has taken second place, well behind preparing for work, in the implicit expectations for schooling and higher education and in the rhetoric of reform. It defies sound reasoning to believe that our casual neglect of inquiry into and conversation about education and schooling in the education of our people has equipped us to conduct the micropolitics better than the macropolitics of schooling. Why should we assume that the causes of the predictable failure of large-scale politically driven school reform will not haunt the politics of small-scale reform?

Certain political realities, assumptions, paradigms, and belief systems will continue to characterize school improvement efforts, regardless of the presence or absence of some genre of "system" beyond the local school. So long as there are tax dollars in any form in support of schools, restraints and controls will accompany their expenditure. Vouchers that follow students from school to school will not change this. There also will be issues and requirements of accountability pertaining to the efficient use of those tax dollars. Regardless of how democratic the symbiotics of local decision making may appear to be, pressure for change will continue to be egocentric, seeking to place various private purposes over the public one. Consequently, there will continue to be need for both civil laws and arbiters of social justice to ensure that the rights and well-being of the larger polity are protected. There is little in our history to support the assumption that micropolitics is more protective of individual liberty and equity than is macropolitics.

The recent history of school decentralization, whether in regard to school reform or functioning, opens to questioning the assumption that this in itself improves the quality of the decisions made. The record of various groups in varying loci coming together in an initial spirit of enthusiasm and goodwill to effect fundamental school change is mixed and largely disappointing. For example, each of the four medium-sized cities receiving substantial funding for reform through the New Futures Initiative started out with enthusiasm in collaboratives involving major elements of their communities. The structural changes in schools that followed appeared not to be guided by educational agendas and left largely untouched school policies and practices.[31] Even with reform efforts close to and involving teachers from local schools, a major part of the net result appears to be added work and stress for teachers seeking to cope with matters that do not support their teaching.

Advocates of dismantling the system argue that the school district is part of the problem; reform initiated there is not sufficiently local. The growing body of research on so-called site-based management makes clear, however, that the shift in the locus of decision making is no panacea either in process or results. Regarding the latter, a link between even intensive teacher participation in decision making in the site-based context and improvement in classroom instruction has not been established.[32] The expectation that the processes will be carried out in a deliberate, productive fashion often turns out to be a fantasy. Micropolitics, like macropolitics, often involves power struggles seeking to place one set of interests over others. If the rhetoric and processes of the larger social context are driven by private purpose—as politically driven school reform has been—it is naive to believe that local rhetoric and processes will be markedly different. Humans are not endowed by nature with associational dispositions. These must be learned.

Strategies and Models of School Change

Three characteristics in particular frustrate school reform and predict its failure. These do not fade away when the process is brought close to the schoolhouse. They arise in large part out of the very concept of reform: Something is wrong and needs fixing. The first characteristic is general failure to recognize that each school is a unique, functioning culture—a political organization that conducts daily business. Within this culture are the subcultures of classrooms, each different and each a political organization. There are no similar cultures and subcultures in the larger community context. Consequently, reform initiatives from outside, even quite close to schools and with teacher representation, are driven by interests and models that portend cultural dissonance. Site-based management by school councils may appear to be a boon to the political life of schools. But increased involvement of parents in selecting principals and teachers does not lessen the intense interest teachers have in this selection process. After listening to teachers talk about the places where they work each day, Seymour Sarason summarized their views:

Each school has its own character and atmosphere. Each school is like a family, and families vary tremendously in their history and in the ties that bind. And like all families, it has its assets and deficits. When you bring in a new teacher or a principal, you are bringing in someone who will affect our lives, positively or negatively, for what can be a long time. As teachers we want a role in shaping our family's destiny. Is it unreasonable to ask for this in a matter that can significantly alter our lives?[33]

Given this sentiment, these teachers might prefer the known of present practices to the unknowns of a shift in power. It is difficult to think of a reform initiative of significance that can proceed successfully without understanding of and attention to the culture of individual schools. The frequent conclusion in school reform that nothing changed implies not just the power of school culture but the ignorance and frequent arrogance of reformers.

A second characteristic that makes failure of school reform predictable is a corollary of the first: linear models narrowly focused on targets derived by guesswork. Test scores are below average; the solution is a longer school day. The children are not reading well enough; clearly, a shift to phonics is called for. High school graduation rates are falling off; there need to be more honors classes and more rigorous tracking of poor students who slow down the more able.

The frequent changes in guesses and proposals during reform eras suggest the frequency of error in both. Teachers find themselves fending off or coping with expectations soon to be replaced with new ones. The energy that might go into serious, long-term renewal is sapped. School people are exhorted to be more businesslike, but good businesses conduct careful analyses of their functioning before effecting change. The circumstances of schooling attract simplistic reform strategies and work powerfully against change. So long as we ignore these circumstances, externally driven reform will be blunted on school and classroom doors, and the necessary internal renewal will proceed not at all or slowly and with great difficulty.

I have described two characteristics that blunt school reform initiatives and eras studied and pronounced ineffective again and again.[34] Figure 4.1 portrays the assumptions of the first: School culture is either ignored or reduced to a linear model of a teacher-student relationship.

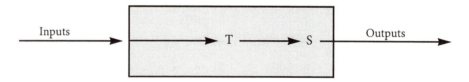

Figure 4.1. School as a Box with Teachers Working on the Learning of Students Inside

Manipulations outside the box are based on guesses about this relationship, are directed toward the teacher to affect the student, and are presumed to make a difference on matters that can be judged on the outside (outcomes such as test scores). In effect, the schoolhouse disappears. A more accurate depiction simply leaves it out, as portrayed in Figure 4.2.

Figure 4.2. School Stripped to Its Essence in Reform Models and Strategies

The conventional reform model depicted is essentially authoritarian: The teacher controls the student in "giving" her or him an education. Because it is authoritarian, the way to strengthen the model is to add the weight of an administrator, the superintendent or principal, or both, as in Figure 4.3.

S or P ───────────► T ───────────► S ───────────► O

Figure 4.3. The Superintendent and/or Principal Work on the Teacher Who Works on the Student to Produce Outcomes

Of course, the model is now weakened because, with rare exceptions, the superintendent (S) and principal (P) who do not teach and who may never have taught the level or subject of the teacher create dissonance for the teacher who is better qualified for her tasks than they are. The Peter Principle one more time. The model ignores the possibility of dissonance arising from a miscellaneous array of cultural factors both inside and outside the school that work on the teacher, the students, their relationships, and the validity and meanings of the outcomes (Figure 4.4).

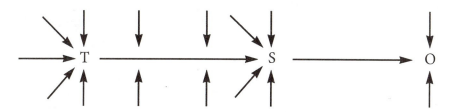

Figure 4.4. Unaccounted-for Dissonance in Simplistic Linear Models of School Reform

It is interesting to note that the bulk of educational research carried out over the years has been and largely still is in service to this model. Quite sophisticated statistical analyses follow paths of relationships, with individuals the unit of selection. Unfortunately, the rigor of the methodology restricts its range, forcing inattention to all but the variables selected for study. Not surprisingly, comparing the impact of the new variable (experimental) with the old (control) has produced a litany of "no significant results." Repeated use of the change model encourages repeated use of the research model. The useful conclusion to be derived from this cycle is that the infusion of single remedies into schools and the study of their effects do not justify the money and time spent.[35]

Overlapping the most recent two or three decades of research focused on individuals that has taught us a great deal about learning, for example, is research focused on classrooms and schools. Regarding our understanding of the latter, Philip Jackson's careful documentation (1968) was both pioneering and seminal.[36] I have referred several times to studies of whole schools, with particular attention to Seymour Sarason's inquiry (1971, revised 1982 and 1996) into the role of school culture in reform and change.[37] There then emerged in the 1990s a stream of articles and books addressed to life in schools, many of them coauthored or written by teachers. The net result is illumination of the school as a complex ecosystem, the specifics of which differ from school to school, within which are classroom subsystems that differ widely in their symbiotics, both within and between schools. In many ways, the schools of the United States are strikingly similar, as are the classrooms in these schools, yet pronounced differences also exist.

Figure 4.5 suggests an entity of nightmarish propensities for the school reformer addicted to linear strategies and remedies. Inside a malleable, penetrable membrane are humans of widely varying ages interacting with one another and with things, following and confronting rules, adjusting to schedules, making thousands of decisions each

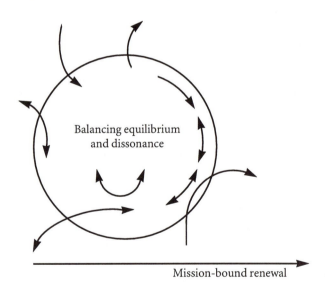

Figure 4.5. A Mission-driven, Responsive, Ecological Model of School Renewal

day, interacting with and reacting to a larger surrounding ecosystem and its expectations. It is a culture that is expected to educate the young while performing a massive custodial function. The custodial function requires equilibrium; education, as I have defined it, produces dissonance. Renewal of the ecosystem necessitates balancing the two in such a way as to be responsive to the immediate context while fulfilling the mission of schooling in a democratic society—a daunting challenge even if this mission were clear and widely agreed upon. The mission is itself a source of dissonance.

I have endeavored to depict in Figure 4.5 both the swirling dynamic character of a complex ecosystem and a concept of steady movement toward greater health—not merely replacing the parts but effecting renewal toward a more robust state of functioning. There are penetrations from the surrounding context; some are internalized so as to effect improvement in the school's culture; some are tossed out; some are shaped to conform to the present state of the culture.

Ignored, attacked, belittled, and unloved, schools decline. Unattended, they decay and perish. Encouraged, supported, and cared for, their health improves. There is as yet no evidence that schools standing alone will thrive and those joined with others in a system will perish. Indeed, such evidence as we have suggests that the systemic differences play a subordinate role to other factors. The problem is that dissatisfaction with the system—derived in part from inflated expectations of what government can and should do to satisfy our private interests—has diverted our attention from the schools we need.

From an Egocentric to an Ecocentric Ethic

Earlier I wrote that three sets of circumstances frustrate school reform and make its failure predictable. The third of these is more pervasive and powerful than the two discussed. It arises out of public perceptions and understandings of what education is and schools are for and the degree to which these have penetrated the eco system of the school. The resulting mirror-image compatibility of context and school has produced a narcissism that blinds us to the possibility of other images: A school is a school is a school.

Consequently, modest changes that enhance the mirror-image according to our established criteria of beauty in schools are appealing: children appearing to be listening attentively to the teacher, a neat and quiet classroom, mathematics taught as a fixed and orderly system, report cards that appear to show precisely how my child is doing, students classified and grouped according to ability, and on and on. There is a widely shared memory of what we construe good schools to have been that shapes our image of what schools should be. The fit between the two is quite precise. Major changes that have the potential for providing conditions that create dissonance in this fit are suspect. The net effect is that the more powerfully educative the proposal for change, the greater its threat to conventional images of what schools are for.

The resulting paradox is that we endlessly restate goals appropriate for education and, therefore, schools addressed to the whole of self-realization and transcendence, while holding much more clearly in mind instrumental expectations tied to our material wants, and then reject practices of potential power in favor of simply improving present ones of little power. In recent years, superintendents of schools have grown increasingly wary about departing from established ways into the minefields of major change. They see around them the terminated contracts of colleagues who have had the temerity to suggest student grouping arrangements to accommodate the well-documented variability in academic achievement among children of the same age and grade, or a multipronged approach to the teaching of reading based on our substantial knowledge of how children learn, or even departure from single textbooks to an array of resource materials. Even to suggest that extant testing procedures and interpretations need to be examined or to bring in a consultant on cooperative learning or how to engage students in problem solving has cost superintendents their jobs. We would do well to look carefully into our images of schooling before decrying the resistance of school administrators to change.

Just as the public image of what schools are and should be is uncomfortably distorted by reflections of alternatives that move across the mirror, the images internal to schools of what is right and good are smudged by these and other intrusions. Teachers have even more reason to be threatened by proposals that will change the established ways of daily work. Significant change not only requires that they learn and do what may be quite novel but also makes them actors in revising parents' scenarios for schooling. It should not surprise us, then, to learn from a growing number of reports and case studies of schools becoming robust and satisfying that a host of supportive factors and extraordinary commitment and effort on the part of principals and teachers carried the renewal effort forward. Most such reports describe or worry about the reality or threat of teacher burnout.

There is profound irony in the observation that the circumstances of teaching serve to maintain rather than dissolve the close relationship between school as it is and school as it should be in the images of schooling both inside the school and in its context. There is neither a solidly grounded teaching profession nor a well-educated professional teaching force to drive the necessary renewing process. Indeed, some recent reform proposals, notably those for a National Board for Professional Teaching Standards,[38] have been advanced with the rhetoric of making teaching a profession. Given the sometimes contemptuous regard for and continued neglect of teacher education, however, there appears to be subconscious agreement that a weak profession is a corollary of the comforting connection between our image of what school has been and our vision of what it should be. The creation of dissonance between the two—a condition necessary to school renewal—requires an exceedingly well-prepared, confident teaching force as well as a highly supportive community context.

The Same but Different

There appears to be an inconsistency between my observation that a school is a school is a school and my preceding argument regarding the uniqueness of school culture and school-to-school differences. The culture of schooling is unique; there is not another like it. And the ecosystems of schools differ; they also have profound similarities. In seeking to unveil some of these differences and similarities, my colleagues and I displayed and analyzed the profiles of a representative sample of elementary and secondary schools in the United States. We clustered vast amounts of data around a dozen or so commonplaces of schools: school climate, class climate, principal-teacher relationships, school-community relationships, teacher-pupil relationships, curricula, instructional methods, and more. The data were then quantified in such way that the schools could be distributed above and below means determined from the sample of which each was a part. Figure 4.6 provides an approximation of this distribution.

The graph reveals a very wide distribution for some characteristics and a lumping of schools quite close together for others. For example, some of the longest bars depict at their upper and lower ends schools that were 2 or 3 standard deviations above or below

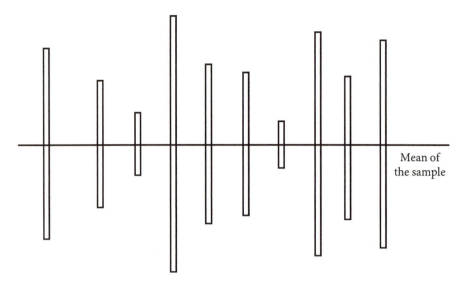

Figure 4.6. Distribution of a Purposefully Representative Sample of Elementary and Secondary Schools on Major Components or Commonplaces

the mean—that is, there were marked school-to-school differences on these elements. In two instances, however, the schools are so closely lumped together as to suggest that, on these elements, a school is a school is a school.

When asked about the differences among these schools, selected by the questioner without preknowledge of the characteristics of any schools in the sample, I respond, "The human connection." The bars depicting the widest dispersions pertain to school climate, class climate, and the sets of relationships (and more) listed above. The two short bars represent our compilations of thousands of data-points pertaining to the schools' curricula and teachers' instructional methods. On what schools are expected to be about, a school is a school is a school. These are the elements that our images of schooling seek to leave intact. These are the elements of schooling that are prescribed and carried forward in the imaging of the public and school personnel alike. These are the elements most resistant to change when school reform initiatives are proclaimed, largely because these initiatives seek to rearrange or reconstruct the system rather than change the circumstances of learning and teaching that shape our images of what schools are and should be.[39]

What I have called the human connection is not prescribed or mandated. Teachers, students, and school patrons need no dismantling of the system to set them free to design the human elements of the schools' ecosystems. They already are free to design them in accordance with associational dispositions that guide their daily lives. Do those most closely connected with schools come together, then, to create civil settings? Clearly, our data revealed extraordinary differences. Some of the schools in our sample had excellent relationships with the families using them, had established caring connections within, took care of their daily business in an orderly way, and were in something resembling a renewing stance.[40] Some were barely connected with the families, marked with dissonance within, and on the verge of falling apart with respect to their daily functioning. The range from good schools to bad schools on the criterion of practicing the democratic individual and community arts was enormous. But who cares whether our schools are cradles of the democratic moral arts? What matters is how they stand and compare on standardized achievement tests, is it not? Or, might there be a correlation between the associational behavior and climate of these schools and their provision of educational conditions and opportunities as earlier defined?

So far, with achievement test scores the conventional output criteria of excellence, the only correlation in which we can have confidence is that of the high association of test scores and the socioeconomic level of a school's clients. Consequently, the driving force in the rhetoric of school reform eras is economic, not educational. We have not yet educated ourselves to value as a high priority the relationship between a civil culture in and around our schools and a civil society.[41] The articulation of this relationship gets lost in the clamor of narrowly instrumental slogans such as "better schools mean better jobs." A letter to the editor of a local newspaper brings its importance into clear, simple focus:

> Our collective tendency . . . to reject school-funding proposals reminds me of a state assembly education committee hearing that I covered as a young reporter in Wisconsin 45 years ago.
>
> The usual line-up of education bureaucrats, school board members, union functionaries and cut-the-taxes advocates was testifying on the annual state aid-to-education bill. At the end of the long afternoon, an elderly woman appeared. She represented only herself, she said, and she didn't think the appropriation was large enough. A puzzled committee chairman tried to find out what her interest really was. No, she said, she'd never been a teacher or served on a school

board; she was just a citizen. Well, the skeptical chairman asked, at least you must have children or grandchildren.

None, she replied, but I have to live with yours.[42]

Correlates of Satisfying Schools

We computed for each school in our sample a "satisfaction index" derived by collating information that implied levels of satisfaction on the part of students, teachers, and parents. None of the questions for which we sought answers addressed satisfaction directly. Rather, satisfaction or dissatisfaction was implied in students' perceptions of whether their school was providing a good education, teachers' views of the professional behavior of their colleagues, parents' opinions regarding the safety of their children and the individual attention they were receiving in the school, and hundreds more reactions to the questions we raised. On a satisfaction scale of 0.00 to 1.00, schools spread out more than 50 points—from the low .20s to the high .70s. Clearly, the schools varied widely on a composite of factors that mattered in the school-based lives of students, teachers, and parents, even though the range in what was being taught and the methods of teaching from school to school was too modest to warrant descriptive differentiation. Schools are places of readily recognizable features that differ widely in the ways the people connected with them *are* with one another.

There is a parallel here in our findings regarding the conduct of schools and Putnam's regarding the conduct of civic affairs in the regions of Italy (Chapter 3). The regions in which local government institutions fulfilled their functions well were those marked by attention to the well-being of the citizens who lived there—regions with a legacy of civic-mindedness and civic participation, Putnam concluded. The schools taking care of their business in self-consciously renewing ways, addressing problems as they arose, keeping parents informed and the environment safe and stable were those producing satisfaction among all three of the groups of people most closely associated with them—schools marked by people respecting and caring for one another and their school.

Our search for possible explanatory demographic factors such as socioeconomic status of the parents revealed only one major connection: None of the largest schools was in the top quartile on the criterion of satisfaction, none of the smallest was in the bottom quartile. It appears that satisfying conditions of schooling are somewhat easier to establish in small schools than in larger ones. This appears to make sense. Small schools are more likely to decrease student-to-teacher anonymity, ease the principals' and teachers' challenge of getting to know parents, make communication simpler, and involve a greater percentage of students and parents in extra-curricular affairs. Recent research reveals benefits to students' academic achievement.[43]

Seeking to threaten, cajole, bribe, or otherwise entice into higher standards of student performance a school that is falling apart or decaying, where human tensions run high, and where there is school-home and parent-teacher distrust is a waste of time. Yet, this is precisely the mode of the linear paradigm of reform that ignores school culture. The first necessity for the new principal at one of Lightfoot's "good" high schools was to get large numbers of truant students off the streets into the school—a goal to challenge students, parents, and teachers alike that the Atlanta school superintendent strongly supported. But this was not the need of all schools in the district or in her sample.

Neither caring, sensitive human connections in the ecosystem of schools nor the priority need for the better health of that ecosystem can be mandated. Likewise, a robust school ecosystem providing education for development of all the "selfs" in its care does not arise out of a diverse array of private egocentric expectations thrust willy-nilly on the principals and teachers. Nor does such an ecosystem arise out of a school culture preoccupied with its own survival. There must be awareness of and commitment to a good larger and more encompassing than the many private ones, the pursuit of which soon becomes self-defeating. There must be understanding of the degree to which the private good is served best when the public good is sustained. Today's schools are torn apart by the intersection of a multiplicity of private expectations. Today's satisfying schools have managed to create an ecosystem that transcends this intersection without denying the private interests it inescapably encompasses. Unfortunately, many of them have compromised their educational mission in deference to practices that retain the comfort of fit between images of schools we remember and what we want them to be—hence the stubborn resistance of curriculum and instruction to change. Innovation is condoned and even encouraged, so long as it does not much threaten the way things are. As one superintendent of schools roused the principals, "Innovate all you want . . . but don't change anything."

Beyond Satisfying Schools

Good schools, according to my priorities, are good places for children and youths to be. But they also are places rich in conditions conducive to education as I have rather repeatedly defined it in preceding chapters. The trouble is that the educational delivery system must be profoundly changed: in the selection and education of its educators, the governance and other mechanisms that support it, the materials and methods of instruction, the orchestration of technological and human teachers, the mix of students and teachers, and on and on. The required changes are alienating. And, ironically, the more schools educate, the more they alienate.

Our work with a group of 18 schools over a period of 6 years convinced us that schools can become good places for children to be through sustained initiatives with this intent in mind. This can be done without radically disturbing the educational delivery system we have. Even the achievement test scores will improve, especially during the later years of a 5-year cycle—and, although there will be modifications in the relationship between these scores and the socioeconomic relationship of the parents, the high correlation will continue.

Getting beyond satisfying schools brings the challenges and risks of their becoming increasingly educative. As stated above, this requires fundamental redesign of the entire delivery system. However, this delivery system cannot be detached from purpose. Present preoccupation with its maintenance is in large part the result of dissonance among conflicting egocentric expectations. The picture at the end of the 20th century is one of small group alliances seeking to become powerful enough to upset equilibrium in their favor. But the resulting disequilibrium merely alerts contradictory factions to actions that maintain the status quo. Rising above the narcissism of the egocentric ethic to one that encompasses the common good is a theme that has challenged human civilization throughout its history. Until schools are guided by such an ethic, they will have great difficulty in, at best, getting beyond the provision of a caring custodial habitat to the cultivation of a caring educational pedagogy. Absent this cultivation, not just the American democracy but the global habitat is at risk.

Stephen John Goodlad assigns to pedagogy the task of nurturing "democratic character," requiring for its development an ethos imbued with an ecocentric (as opposed to egocentric) environmental ethic:

The nurturing of democratic character is much of what schooling is about. But such schooling requires a civic society and . . . our society has fallen victim to a certain mythology about what it means to be human and which has helped give rise to a set of socioeconomic pressures that are fundamentally anti-democratic in nature. . . . The ideas and themes embodied in an ecocentric environmental ethic may provide a context within which we can begin anew the task of educating for a democratic character.[44]

CHAPTER 5

Education and
Its Conditions

It is commonplace for human beings to transpose thoughts to the degree that the language of their formulation is mistaken for the realities described. This is particularly so for thoughts of things perceived to be good, just, or beautiful, often extolled in the environment. The condition described as democracy fits this criterion, a condition frequently associated with education in our discourse. Consequently, it is easy to shrug off even carefully reasoned warnings regarding shortcomings in the people's nurturing of both democracy and education. The critic may be regarded as a crank consumed with thoughts of imminent doomsday.

Awareness of this context contributed significantly to my decision, advanced in the Preface, to use a spiraling approach to the development of just a few ideas in praise of education as well as the dangers to it that arise primarily out of indifference. This chapter continues to cultivate these ideas, this time from the perspective of *conditions* necessary to the nurturing of education in a democratic society. The intent is to sensitize readers to the hard fact that celebrating belief in education is a far cry from putting in place the conditions under which it flourishes. Celebrating education comes easily; fostering it requires a sustained commitment to the public and not merely the private good.

Two characteristics dominate our thought and discourse regarding education. The first pertains to goals, the second to individuals doing or being done to. The conditions necessary to education's nurturing surface much less readily and, usually, with more accompanying controversy when they do enter the conversation.

It is the rare schoolteacher who does not experience several times in a decade being part of an exercise in stating educational goals. And it is the rare group of teachers that fails to come up with rather close agreement on a dozen or so in an hour or less. Almost invariably, the goals are stated in the form of understandings, skills, and attitudes to be acquired by individuals, from those of rather immediate, practical utility to those of more abstract universality. The content of discourse becomes more vague and varied if it turns to what students and teachers must do.

When education is addressed as a field of study, the individual is the prime unit of selection. In Chapter 1, I pointed out that the faculties in schools and colleges of education are comprised mainly of members whose focus is on the individual as the unit of selection. Their studies of individuals constitute a very large proportion of the educational research literature. Those historians, philosophers, anthropologists, and sociologists who address the larger issues of context are in short supply. In Chapter 4, I noted the degree to which policymakers persevere in their focus on outcomes and the individuals who are to produce or achieve these outcomes but commonly are mute with respect to the necessary conditions.

Education is a handy virtue to promulgate when the obligation to become educated falls on another, as is the case when we set educational goals for the young and then ignore what all of us must do to ensure their attainment. We can content ourselves with faith in the individual human spirit—"faith, which can wait patiently, without asking too many questions."[1] Virtue readily becomes burden and faith insufficient nourishment, however, when education is promulgated as a collective responsibility as is necessarily the case when closely tied to democracy and especially to the development of a democratic character guided by an ecocentric environmental ethic.

We dare not wait patiently or even impatiently for educational goals and individual enterprise to satisfy our educational needs and aspirations. At least three sets of demanding contextual conditions are necessary to the education that individual and collective democratic character require. First, education must be regarded and protected as an inalienable right. Second, teaching must be included in the definition of and expectations for responsible citizenship. Third, the risk-laden nature of teaching and the implications thereof must be raised to and kept at a high level of cultural visibility.

We are becoming increasingly and painfully aware of what the ecocentric environmental ethic demands of democratic character. We must confront also what the development of this character requires of the contextual ethic: education as individual right, maximum opportunity for access to education, public responsibility and accountability for the conditions necessary to education. In this educational house, no rooms are reserved for villain theorists. We are all culpable for shortcomings and misdeeds in the cultivation of education.

Education as Inalienable Right

I began Chapter 1 with a long quote from Donald Vandenberg in support of my argument regarding the ubiquitous character of education. He places education at the center of human experiences. His vision of the centrality and comprehensiveness of education brings with it a human rights ethic: ". . . the basic moral obligation to maintain and enhance human dignity results in the human rights to equal freedom, equal consideration, and brotherly/sisterly love. Each of these human rights is a universal obligation, or categorical imperative."[2] The ubiquitous presence of education in human affairs does not fulfill this obligation. Equal access requires statutory laws to establish a community under law, according to Vandenberg: "The classroom as a community of scholars under law dedicated to maximizing the learning of each student should be structured by the human rights to freedom, equal consideration, and brotherly and sisterly love to establish dialogical relations among students in an atmosphere of affection, so students obey the rules of equal freedom out of love, trust, and a sense of fairness and find some pleasure in doing so."[3]

The language is not unlike that of Johannes Althusius four centuries ago (cited in Chapter 3). It is far removed from today's political rhetoric of school reform; debate over school choice; national, state, and local discussion of performance standards; expectations for teaching and teacher education; and, indeed, most discussions of what education and schools are for. Vandenberg's book, *Education as a Human Right*, is subtitled *A Theory of Curriculum and Pedagogy*. Hardly anything in the curricular and pedagogical preparation of teachers, in what and how teachers teach, or in the daily conduct of most schools aligns with Vandenberg's classroom educational community.

Vandenberg's conception of education as a human right—to be guided by moral ethic, protected under law as a universal obligation, and conducted so as to enhance the human dignity in oneself and others in such way that it is "a pleasure to do the right thing"[4]— and today's public educational discourse are a vast chasm apart. Yet, if a dozen or so of those thinkers of the past who probed the connection between education and human well-being were to be seated today around the seminar table, they would enter easily into conversation with Mr. Vandenberg as though it were their daily habit. If education is necessary to the making of a public, as Walter Feinberg suggests,[5] and this public is to be the civil one for which Benjamin Barber argues ("that unites the virtue of the private sector—liberty—with the virtue of the public sector—concern for the general good"),[6] we face a mighty chasm to be bridged. In its face, today's babble over school reform finds kinship with the quacking of mallard ducks in a puddle.

The problem a large part of today's public would be likely to have with Vandenberg (and the others at the table engaged comfortably in conversation with him) might—but must not—be shrugged off as one of language. Language articulates concepts and ideas. Those of Vandenberg are not merely alternative paths through a familiar part of the forest. His are of a part less traversed. The alternative paths about which his colleagues might agree or disagree rarely intersect with those of the familiar part. Those in the familiar part are hurrying along the footpaths anxious to reach gratification at the end—worrying, as Tocqueville observed (Chapter 2), that they might not be on the quickest route there. Those on the paths less traveled have no such delayed gratification in mind. They are too busily observing (and, we trust, enjoying) "that existing things are valuable because they have their own qualities and that one ought to learn to value all things by becoming aware of their qualities."[7] On coming out of the woods, they turn back on another path for still more educational experiences and for reflection on them (possibly in company with Aristotle, Bacon, Whitehead, Dewey, and contemporaries such as Maxine Greene, Robert Westbrook, Donna Kerr, and Nel Noddings). Asked whether they enjoyed their seminar in the woods, a member of one returning party responded, "Very enlightening. And every time we went down a path, we met John Dewey coming back."

Such is what education is. But it must not be the privilege of just a few. Until recently in human history, the journey was for the scholar cloistered in an abbey or university, and regarded as wasted on the "simple folk." The democratic ethic and the democratic character require otherwise. "The great country, the great society, the great community is, first of all, the well-educated country, the learned society, the community of excellence. This nation knows it, proclaims it, even rhapsodizes about it. Then it busies itself with other matters."[8]

Civic Ethic and Civil Law

The educative context is a tenuous resource, subject to erosion, corruption, and destruction. Its protection and nourishment depend on both an individual and a collective ethic of a sort envisioned in democratic character. Education is corrupted when viewed only as a sequence of carefully chosen contingencies directed toward personal gratification. With everyone competing for their own ends and means, the context is lacerated. Turning to the analogy of the forest once again, it becomes a clear-cut. Everyone loses. With a single series of contingencies prescribed and successful progression through them required for the enjoyment of family, work, and freedom, the landscape is marred by many crippled, unfulfilled selves. And the part of the forest that might have nurtured their individuality disappears from collective consciousness—life's curriculum narrows.

The idea of education through *paideia* as a transition from childhood to adulthood is very old. According to Philippe Ariès, it was largely lost in the Middle Ages, with children recognized soon after weaning as the natural companions of adults. By the 16th and especially the 17th century, however, a positive moralization of society was taking place that led to recognition of the importance of education. Increasingly, the teaching of religious orders such as the Jesuits and the Oratorians was addressed to young people and their parents. "This literature, this propaganda, taught parents that they were spiritual guardians, that they were responsible before God for the souls, and indeed the bodies too, of their children. Henceforth it was recognized that the child was not ready for life, and that he had to be subjected to a special treatment, a sort of quarantine, before he was allowed to join the adults."[9] The moral ethic transmitted to the family required the training of all children as preparation for later life. Apprenticeship to family life was not sufficient; the special training would be provided by a school—"an instrument of strict discipline, protected by the law-courts and the police-courts."[10]

Ariès goes on to point out how this family responsibility, joined with the school, contributed to middle-class moral ascendancy that combined a desire for privacy with a craving for identity—and a shrinking from the "promiscuity" of the sociable community. Schools formed part of the emerging class system, coming to be in time part of its sustenance. This European evolution was well along before the era of massive emigration to the new American colonies.

This concept of a formal system for "civilizing" the young carried over into the New World where the upper-class householders

of the early towns feared the emergence of an uncivil rabble, igno-
rant of the laws of the land and the principles of religion. The schools
for which the landed were taxed were not for *their* children—they
had other alternatives—but for community well-being.[11] The purpose of the early American schools was, then, essentially a public
one. There appears to have been no thought to education as a right,
a civic ethic designed to ensure maximum cultivation of the self.
As we know, there emerged a compulsory system of formal schooling, with the right to private schooling preserved, presumably to help
preserve the class system that paralleled the European version.

The increasing shift from an agrarian to an industrial demand
for workers, accelerating in the second half of the 19th century, that
sought more and more from the schools, contributed significantly
to the equating of education and schooling in people's minds. The
accompanying school reform rhetoric of increased personal efficiency (ability to participate in the economy) and increased societal
efficiency (less crime and better prepared workers)[12] also elevated
the private purpose of schooling while emphasizing education as
instrument rather than as end in its own right. As so often is the
case, reform begets counterreform. The machinelike system of older
children monitoring the learning routines of the younger, introduced early in the 1800s by Joseph Lancaster,[13] and the age-graded
pattern that subsequently hardened into place became grist for the
mills of reformers who viewed education as the cultivation of
morality.

It appears that the 13 colonies that entered into a loose union
of independence in 1776, and in 1787 framed a document for a
"more perfect union," saw no need to guarantee education as an
ethic of civic responsibility and a civil right. Home and church would
take care of individual virtue; schools, such as there were, a short
rite of passage into adulthood. All three institutions and one's lot
in life were in God's hands. To the extent that schools were to go
beyond the teaching of reading, writing, and figuring, it was to the
development of character in God's image. But for the workers of
developing cities of the 19th century, such as New York, Philadelphia, and Boston, there was a growing vision of a better life on this
earth, not just in the hereafter.

For some, the better life envisioned included more than work
and more than the entitlements of work. How fascinating it would
be today to sit in on the meetings of the Working Man's Party of
Philadelphia and of Boston, circa 1830. In 1831, Stephen Simpson
attempted to capture the central theme of the former as follows:

"Nothing is so essentially connected with the wealth of nations, and the happiness of the people, as the proper cultivation, expansion, and discipline of the popular mind. Upon this depends not only the amount of public virtue and happiness—but the aggregate of industry, ingenuity, temperance, economy, and vigour."[14] Simpson set development of the mind as an educational end in its own right, while making no separation of the benefit mutually to the individual and society. Reflecting still on the party's stance, he pronounced education to be the right of all, rich and poor (with the rich paying more for its nourishment), to be protected as a constitutional liberty: "Indeed, to conceive of a *popular government* devoid of a system of *popular education*, is as difficult as to conceive of a civilized society destitute of a *system of industry*."[15] Unlike so many political pronouncements of today, education was not to be subservient to industry; the two were to exist independently, side by side.

In Boston, at about the same time, the platform put forward by the Working Man's Party made this distinction very clear, stating the right to work and the right to education as separate planks.[16] In writings of the party, educational capital is treated virtually as a property right, to be kept maximally open to all and protected by the assumption of both individual and collective responsibility. The party was so worried about unequal acquisition of financial capital creating unequal access to educational capital and this inequality being passed from generation to generation that it proposed enrollment of all children in boarding schools at a very young age. In this way, life's playing field would be leveled, at least early on in a child's development. Once again we see in the varied stirrings of American democracy a desire to break away from the European pattern of simultaneous class and educational advantage—a cause championed by the labor movement on both continents.

In their work, historians eschew the recent past in favor of gaining the perspective of elapsed time. Perhaps, in a quarter or half a century, we will have a definitive, balanced account of the role of education and particularly schooling in the century and a half preceding the year 2000. There is sharp divergence in the two major stories now available. One is recounted each year in thousands of high school and college graduation addresses. It is a story of free and universal schooling (with *education* often substituted for *schooling*), available to American-born and immigrant alike, tied to personal prosperity and happiness in a context of liberty and freedom. The message of the commencement speaker is one of giving back in appreciation of these bounties. The expectancy of still better things to come is tempered by that of responsibility to preserve the democracy that has provided so much.

Until recently, the other story simply was not the stuff of graduation ceremonies. Unlike having to invite the inevitably inebriated Uncle Harry to the annual family gathering, inviting a revisionist speaker to give the commencement address was avoidable—and still is not a common occurrence. We are aware that there has not been equal access to schools that are commonly good and that financial capital and access to the best schools of choice go hand in hand.[17] We are becoming aware that conditions widely regarded as correlated with access to knowledge—such as instructional materials and well-prepared teachers—are far more associated with schools attended by the affluent than by the poor.[18] Even when the student population in a given school is diverse with respect to financial capital, race, and other characteristics, we learn that it commonly is organized so as to ensure that the students who have enjoyed the most comfortable home environments for the longest periods of time will be found disproportionately in classes featuring the "best" knowledge, the most experienced teachers, and the most supportive educational climate.[19] And then we find that, for many parents of those so advantaged, school reform means the return of tax dollars for essentially private schools of choice immune from the persuasions of egalitarian-minded reconstructionists.

Without the luxury of a historical perspective tempered and enlightened by the passage of time, an observer might well conclude that the American democracy had acquired by the year 2000 what the European middle class had envisioned a couple of centuries earlier as ideal, as a moral ethic: schools "protected by the law-courts" and considerable protection from the "promiscuity" of the sociable community, either through choice of a community accessible to the more affluent or a degree of social class segregation effected through the internal organization of schools. The observer might note also, however, the nagging of another moral ethic: the historical promise of a dream to be realized by all, a dream depicting a civil rather than a promiscuous community.

The concluding decades of the 20th century were accompanied by increased blurring of the lines between the two stories of education and schooling in the United States referred to above. Increasingly, the disadvantaged circumstances of the most vulnerable segments of society and the responsibility of the advantaged become a sobering part of graduation rhetoric. The promises of the American Dream not realized by many people in the 20th century were put forward as an agenda for the 21st. As for the 20th, the critical role of education was placed at the center of the agenda for the 21st century.

The goal of schooling protected by law was attained. Attesting to this are PL 94–142, the Education for All Handicapped Children Act of 1975, and PL 101–476, the Individuals With Disabilities Act of 1990. The value claims of these federal enactments are "that all handicapped children have a right to a free and appropriate public education, that the state must identify, locate, and evaluate all children in need of special education, that pupils with disabilities must be educated to the extent appropriate with their nondisabled peers."[20] In effect, the right proclaimed by and for the nation is the right to schooling.

Ironically, the fact of the law regarding access to schooling attests also to the immaturity of our ethic with respect to education as a right. Halfway through the 20th century, the United States Supreme Court affirmed not only the right but also the necessity of its availability to all on equal terms.[21] Arguably, the Justices had in mind "schooling," and certainly issues of access to schooling dominated the post-1954 Court decision scene for decades to follow. Julie K. Underwood has effectively pointed out the persistence of unequal terms even as school districts struggled to implement the law. She defined and documented three sets of conditions producing unequal access to the learning provided by schools: those innate to children, those created by environmental conditions, and those resulting from states' actions and omissions.[22]

These conditions did not go unaddressed or unpublicized. The growing body of literature on individual differences could not be described as mainstream but did get into the education curricula of teachers and parent study groups. For a time, states legislated and funded so-called compensatory education programs for the disadvantaged. James B. Conant's depiction of gross differences between urban and suburban provisions for schools as "social dynamite" was widely covered by the press.[23] And, of course, mandated busing as an effort to equalize school access was extensively used and passionately argued.

Clearly, many policies and practices of the concluding decades of the 20th century attested to a maturing of the nation's ethic with respect to the right to *schooling. Brown v. Board of Education* established the right to attend, PL 94–142 the right to a personalized program. The policies and practices attest also to the nation's difficulty with the concept of *education* as a right to be protected and advanced as an individual and a collective good. The chasm between this concept—no stranger to the celebration of democracy—and reality remained strong and deep.

The question as to whether we want a mature civic ethic that transcends schooling to encompass education rises to significance alongside the question of whether such is attainable. Of course, wanting it is essential to attaining it.

Teaching Democratic Character

The democratic credo of freedom and justice for all has carried us a long way in providing legal protection for the individual. It has not yet brought us to a mature civic ethic regarding individual opportunity in spite of the degree to which individual liberty has been at the core of this credo. This is critically important work still in progress. Equally important and recently more neglected is attention to collective democratic character—to the making of civil communities. Caring, interpersonal symbiotics are a necessary part of such but not sufficient. There must be a civic cultural conscience. The contrast between ideal and reality is great:

> Our culture does not nourish that which is best or noblest in the human spirit. It does not cultivate vision, imagination, or aesthetic or spiritual sensitivity. It does not encourage gentleness, generosity, caring, or compassion. Increasingly in the late twentieth century, the economic-technocratic-static worldview has become a monstrous destroyer of what is loving and life-affirming in the human soul.[24]

This surround teaches. It teaches with all the resources of modern communication at its disposal. Its seductive enticements pull schools more and more into an ethos that has little to do with the cultivation of a civil society. The long-range dangers of this trajectory may nag at those propelling it but are outweighed by fear of the short-range consequences of reaching for the throttle. Since the trains going down the tracks are in intense competition, who will be the first to reach? And who will follow?

Shaping the Teaching Context

At the time of this writing, there is growing conversation about the need to nourish a civil infrastructure. Robert Putnam's piece on the decline in bowling leagues as one of many signs of decline in the horizontal relationships he correlates with social and political democracy (Chapter 3) induced surprisingly widespread discourse and some sharp disagreement. In commending the community activities that bring people together and the accompanying chats, David Mathews notes that these must have particular characteristics in order to strengthen public life—"they have to build public capital rather than purely social capital . . . people must have opportunities to engage in a larger conversation about the well-being of the community as a whole."[25]

The good society is shaped by the beliefs and actions of its citizens. More accurately, the good society is shaped by what and how the people teach one another. Today, much of that teaching carries with it a business-economic ethic in a context of declining opportunities for the "larger conversation" Mathews advocates. Absent the places and the associations of healthy public life, there is likely to be little conversation about the content of what individuals hear and see, much of the time alone. The issue of learning alone—a central promise of modern technology—looms larger than that of bowling alone (a major message in Putnam's metaphorical use of the bowling example).

Since human beings are in some way connected with much in the community that teaches, a first necessity in creating a broadly educative infrastructure is to arouse a consciousness for responsible teaching among all those who teach or potentially could teach. I sketched the possibilities in Chapter 3 and shall not elaborate here. The issue is how to initiate public conversations about education and teaching. Ironically, the fact of our tendency to equate education and even teaching with schooling suggests schooling as the propitious entry point.

What has been described in recent years as a struggle for the soul of the American public school is an asset in seeking to move toward markedly elevated public awareness of the need to teach one another the meaning of collective as well as individual democratic character. The natural questions for the necessary conversation are whether schools have a public purpose and, if so, what it is. If schools have a public purpose, then David Mathews provides in the title of his little book the title of the next question: *Is There a Public for Public Schools?*

Should belief in schools as instruments for satisfying the nation's needs for humanpower dominate our culture, we will continue to fashion schools less and less in the image of the rhetoric that characterized graduation exercises for most of the 20th century. Should the conversation advance the conclusion that schools must be positioned to advance the democratic moral arts, surely we will come to realize that educating for democracy cannot be left to schools only moderately redesigned or to schools alone. Rather, the development of democratic character must come to be routinely fostered by the culture. The agenda for getting there embraces all of us.

Agenda for Education in a Democracy

The concluding decade of the 20th century was marked by a rather rasping debate over public schooling. Very little of it addressed what education is and what schools are for. Much of it began with the assumption that our system of public schooling had failed us, not that the people might have failed it. Data-based refutations of this assumption, several of them cited here in earlier chapters, did little to blunt it, particularly for those individuals and segments of the population seeking private schools of choice supported by the public purse. Since these refutations came primarily from educational researchers, their reports were accused of being self-serving and, therefore, of being highly selective in their choice of data. Indeed, some of those educators so charged were accused of defending the status quo, even if their presentations of data were accompanied or followed by solid proposals for improving and even changing the schools we have. This kind of debate does not readily lead to serious consideration of and action on alternatives. The challenge is to inform the debate in the hope of pushing it toward more productive channels. The danger is, of course, the power of private interest.

The decade was marked also by two streams of conversation, only occasionally joined, regarding growing threats to the future of our democracy, on one hand, and of our children, on the other. First Lady Hillary Rodham Clinton provided strong rhetorical moral support for those in the vanguard of championing children's rights. President Clinton launched a campaign exhorting the media to set aside time for programs of interest to and in the best interests of children. A next step, of course, is to raise the moral conscience of those who determine the messages and entertainment intended for adults but that readily reach children as well. Mary Catherine Bateson saw in the larger social ecology the opportunity to educate children for the teaching of the total family—a concept that some parents fear—and provided compelling reasons why parents can no longer be regarded as adequate spokespersons for their children's future.[26]

Also in the 1990s, professors of education, philosophy, and political science, in particular, stirred once again the never-settled theme of balance between freedom and responsibility and the critical role of education in the democratic duality. Several devoted comprehensive volumes to what John Dewey had to say on the issues. A rash of books and articles addressed character development, civic education, and educating the democratic mind in the schools.

Colleagues and I participated, seeking particularly to ground the debate over schooling in the common good rather than in private purpose. In this, we were not pioneers. We were revisiting and recasting a recurring part of the human conversation. It is interesting to note the parallelism in thinking that occurs even when there appears not to be any direct communication among the conversationalists. Perhaps it was the imminent conclusion of a tumultuous century that stimulated so much related thinking about the American democracy as a work in progress and the educational agenda necessary to its further advancement.

Even though the agenda of developing individual and collective moral character transcends schools, it encompasses them. As Barber notes (in the quotation above), we rhapsodize the highest expectations and then busy ourselves with other matters. The connecting of education and democracy as a moral imperative for the schools is not clearly articulated in federal, state, and local policies. When some schools seek to take patriotic rhetoric seriously, they often are attacked for usurping family prerogatives and neglecting their responsibility for teaching "the basics." This narrowing of school role reinforces rote learning and reduces teaching to the mechanics of instruction. The concept of nurturing the self in a richly layered context of teaching and learning languishes and frequently is negated.

Inquiries conducted with colleagues over several years laid bare the gulf between the nation's investment in the idea of education and wholehearted provision of the necessary conditions, as well as much of the accompanying dissonance. The slippage from rhetoric to reality is abrupt, even when policymakers begin to put substance into their expectations for schools. This substance consists not of the infrastructure an enlightened nation must provide to ensure education as an individual right and a civic necessity. It prescribes instead what children must be able to do. The prescriptions are largely silent on what parents, neighbors, teachers, and the state are to do to fulfill the moral imperative that is so explicitly in the story of graduation ceremonies and so absent in the story of politically driven school reform agendas.

My colleagues and I concluded that, somewhere in the educational woods, the schooling enterprise took a wrong turn and found a path strewn with billboards advertising humanpower needs and offering rewards for school-based training. The language connoted an educational journey, but the graphics bespoke personal gratification in the ending, not fulfillment and satisfaction in the taking. John Dewey was nowhere to be seen. Perhaps he was thinking in a glade somewhere else in the forest.

There was little we liked about this path. The history of its making revealed a story that diverged sharply from its promise—a familiar source of disillusionment. We mapped an alternative specifically for teacher educators, setting forth 19 sets of conditions for its engineering and maintenance.[27] The conditions are those of moral stewardship on the part of educational institutions for the educational journey of those who teach our children in schools—a markedly different journey from the one that, in our negligence, we have provided for the nation's teachers.

We realized that laying down the path was only a beginning. The potholes, erosions, and collapsed bridges on the one commonly traveled were so obviously in need of repair that more user-friendly possibilities readily came to mind. The larger issues for which the existing conditions provided little help pertained to the educational encounters to be experienced along the way. For answers we sought out John Dewey and like-minded thinkers of the past and present who have provided seminal insights into what education and the good society are and how democratic character is developed. Out of these inquiries came a mission for schools and those who are their moral stewards in civil communities.

The cornerstone of this mission is enculturation of the young in and for a social and political democracy. This enculturation at each stage of self-transcendence requires increasing ability to derive meanings from the culture so as to be able to participate fully in the human conversation, an ability derived in part from liberal studies. The teaching required of adults is risk-laden and must be honed through lifelong formal, nonformal, and informal education and acquisition of pedagogical arts. The ultimate in self-transcendence here on this earth is identification with and responsibility for the entirety of our surround, that is, the development of the ecocentric environmental ethic Bateson implies. Those teachers charged with the education of the young in educational institutions carry special moral responsibility. However, the self-authorized constitute our largest teaching force and share this responsibility.

Mission serves like the polar star to help keep one on course. One need only glimpse a mission from time to time if one's surround is imbued with its essence. For example, there is little need to invoke the importance of caring for one another if caring for one another is as present in what we do as is the air we breathe. In Chapter 3, I referred to Dewey's conception of an educational environment bespeaking the very attributes desired in the learners—for instance, the attributes of democratic character. By contrast, the teaching of mathematics, for example, as an arbitrary, inflexible, closed system is reflective of the dictates of an authoritarian régime.[28]

For many people, "mission" denotes the destination, not the journey. Hence, the end justifies the means for attaining it, and efficiency becomes the major criterion for comparing and choosing paths to the destination. I argue quite differently. The means must satisfy the same moral criteria embedded in the ends. The democratic cornerstone of our mission reminds us of our responsibility to one another and the cosmos, providing a sense of belonging together to things beyond our immediate selves. Individual identity with a universal whole was viewed by Pierre Teilhard de Chardin as the source of humankind's continuity or immortality.[29]

Our mission embraced both schools and the education of those authorized to teach in them. To the cornerstone of enculturating the young into a social and political democracy we added that of gaining access to the necessary knowledge and then, for teachers, those of caring pedagogy and moral stewardship. The four-part mission lacks the specificity of an agenda. It is intended to serve as a kind of compass to keep travelers from turning unwittingly toward paths marked by those blinking neon signs. The 19-point agenda provides the stepping stones for sure-footed walking.

The journey is not to be, then, a quick run along the shortest linear route but one of reflection and conversation through complex physical and social environments. The theoretical biologist, Robert Rosen, put forward the case for humans' requiring for their self-development a rich sensory input.[30] The educational journey of self-transcendence requires a context that cultivates the individual, community, and humankind moral arts. At the time of this writing, 16 settings in 14 states embracing 34 colleges and universities, over 100 school districts, and approximately 400 partner or professional development schools (with this number growing steadily) are formally committed to advancing this agenda through the National Network for Educational Renewal (NNER).[31]

Even though the agenda apparently had appeal, it was the mission that became increasingly compelling. By the mid-1990s, educators in the NNER settings and beyond spoke frequently about "the conversation"—an expanding conversation regarding the agenda's moral grounding. What it implied for the role of teachers and teacher educators resonated with the motivations that had attracted many of them into teaching in the first place. Some of this initial idealism—much of it lost over time to its poor fit with regularities of schooling—was rekindled. There was a growing perception, too, that the mission of just two comprehensive expectations for schools encompassing the individual self and the civil community offered hope of reducing the plethora of often-conflicting private purposes tearing the fabric of the public school system.

A shadow over this educational renewal initiative addressed simultaneously to schools and institutions of higher education was the danger perceived to reside in the absence of informed conversation in the general public regarding the relationship between a robust, renewing democracy and education and, within this relationship, the role of schools in creating a responsible public. Whereas, earlier, the worry had been the daunting nature of the agenda and perhaps some self-doubts about advancing it, the major challenge perceived for the concluding years of the century was that of getting much broader participation in the conversation. The success of schools in shaping democratic character depends on the extent to which the surround is imbued with this expectation. A society that self-consciously tends to the tenets of social and political democracy supports schools that serve democratic public purpose.

Responsibility for the Necessary Conditions

I have argued that the nourishment of a democracy that fulfills its promise to all of us requires a comprehensive educative infrastructure. The promise will go unfulfilled if we simply assign responsibility to schools and go about our private purposes. But I have argued also that getting our heads straight about the public purpose of schooling for shaping democratic character pushes us toward a better understanding of what education is and perhaps even a strengthened resolve to weave this understanding into the educative surround that is always teaching something. In fact, an agenda for school-based education in a democracy has the potential for sensitizing the polity to the educational conversations, policies, and practices the well-being of civil societies requires. The teaching surround not only becomes safer for the teaching of democracy in schools but also an ally in forwarding the agenda.

Commitment

A fundamental condition for schools, if they are to serve this public purpose, is clear enunciation of it. The vagaries of partisan politics, often geared to estimates of what will sell at the next election rather than to the public good, frequently serve to obfuscate the message. As discussed in Chapter 4, politically driven school reform tends to concentrate on reformulating outcomes likely to be viewed as attractive to political action committees and groups of voters. Consequently, there is at best only short-term interest in putting in place the conditions necessary to producing these changing outcomes. With respect to schooling, short-term omissions have long-term effects. For schools to advance their democratic public purpose, both the expectation for and the conditions necessary to the development of democratic character must persist generation after generation.

The ends put forward on the outside for schools—almost invariably in the form of outcomes such as standards to be achieved—are perceived almost invariably on the *inside* as inputs competing with other inputs. Figure 4.5 (Chapter 4) sought to depict schools as the cultural realities they are, coping with an array of inputs, using some, rejecting others. Until expectations become part of this cultural process, they are meaningless or, at most, nuisances. Politically driven reform expectations must be seriously regarded as an input to be reckoned with or they remain impotent phrases. Politicians appear to be sufficiently aware of this to resort to carrot-and-stick forms of motivation: merit pay for evidence of "improved" outcomes, financial awards for the performance of whole schools, assumption of direct state management of an entire district declared academically bankrupt, and so on.

Figure 5.1 modifies the conventional model of school reform depicted in Figure 4.1 so as to convert the stated outcomes into part of the total array of inputs. They may make it into the gray box of the school (for example, they might appear on the agenda of faculty meetings), but this does not necessarily get them into the gray

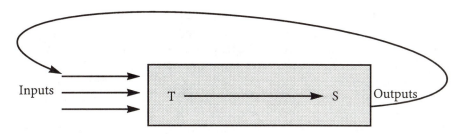

Figure 5.1. Formally Stated Outputs for Schools Competing with Other Inputs for Entry Into the School

boxes of the classrooms whose membranes are much less penetrable. Teachers are not waiting passively for them. Rather, they are busily using the inputs of their own years of schooling and teaching, the texts adopted for the grades, and the district course of studies[32] while perhaps making some pedagogical adjustments to the rising parental call for more attention to the basics. The chances of inputs finding their way into this teaching-learning relationship if they do not reinforce it are slim, indeed. School reform expectations may gain rhetorical recognition in the school only to die at the classroom door. Even when school principals seriously seek organizational changes in their schools, for example, teachers usually regard them coolly unless they perceive connections with daily instruction.

Although Figure 4.5 and the narrative surrounding it in Chapter 4 depicted the cultural reality of schools that improvement initiatives must seek to understand and address, it is incomplete. Figure 4.6 revealed the lack of variation in the curriculum and teaching of classrooms, regardless of the wide school-to-school variations in what I referred to as "the human connection." Whether we compare the classrooms of 50 years ago with those of today or those of the United States with those of Australia, France, Israel, or Japan, there are similarities sufficient to support the observation, "A school is a school is a school." There is a hard core of teaching and learning mathematics, science, history, geography, reading, and writing conducted in a context of human relationships of considerable variability. And it is fascinating to note that, in elementary schools of the United States, the emphasis on a hard core of reading and mathematics is not diminished even in classrooms where the sloppy use of time results in shortchanging other subjects.[33]

These realities point to the need for adding to Figure 4.5 in such way as to embed the classroom boxes deeply inside the school's ecosystem. Figure 5.2 attempts to do this with one classroom proxy for all. I have retained the hard classroom walls because this is close to reality. I have not connected inputs into the school directly to the classroom because they are transposed if they get there at all. But I have added inputs that come directly into the classroom (for example, from parents, often through their children), outputs from the classroom going directly outside of the school (usually to parents and, again, often through the children), and inputs that come into the classroom only to go out again in a direct exchange.

There are two profound implications here for the role of schools in the agenda for education in a democracy. First, the commonality of schools virtually everywhere is the hard core of the classrooms (no matter how much connected with the information highway and the worldwide web of electronic communications). The nations of the world set academic expectations for the schools to be carried out in these classrooms. The classroom box is virtually filled with

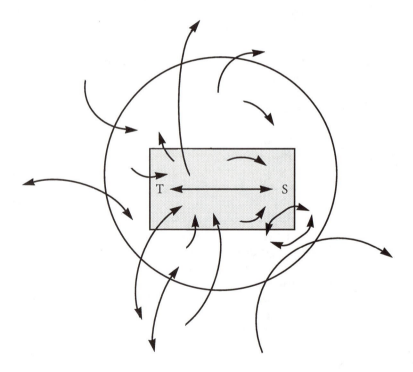

Figure 5.2. The Classroom Box with Its Interactions as the Hard Core of the School's Ecosystem

inputs already in place: teachers and students. The space for additional inputs is very small and hotly competed for, especially in democratic societies. James Coleman's widely circulated conclusion regarding the degree to which children's own inputs fill up the space stimulated parents' interest in seeking out schools they thought likely to have classrooms filled with students carrying much educational capital with them.[34] Parents tended to view his later conclusions regarding the superiority of private schools as a product of their being private rather than their being smaller and characterized by more educational capital in the classroom space occupied by children.[35] Coleman's tempering of his initial top placement of students' input over teachers' added later support to the proposition that the weight of the latter could be substantially increased. Ironically, as I already have stated, both the importance of the teaching profession and the selection and education of teachers, the major input along with students in the classroom, have been seriously undernourished in our nation.

The single most promising way to improve what teachers routinely do, which squares with what most of their patrons want them to do, is to put into the classrooms teachers already deeply immersed in the what and how of doing it, who have learned their subject matter once for themselves and once for teaching it to others, as well as at least a half-dozen ways of engaging their students with it. And then we need to fill the classroom space not taken up with these teachers and their students so that everything in it represents for teaching and learning the equivalent of what our very best businesses require for their making and selling. Corporate executives: Educators are not interested in hearing how you do it; they want what you do it with. Leaving the gates to teaching loosely latched for retirees from business and the military whose college diplomas have faded over time and whose pedagogical preparation for the classroom was acquired in a 6-week workshop is not part of the input that matches academic output in the equation. If what is in the classroom constitutes the hard core of the traditionally implicit output of academic learning, let us be sure that the necessary conditions of teachers and teaching are commonly in place there.

The second implication of Figure 5.2 pertains to what surrounds the classroom nucleus. Here is where we find the major school-to-school differences. And, interestingly, these differences tend to characterize the classrooms and the surround both internal and external to the individual school. Schools with trusting, caring relationships among the teachers and between the principals and the teachers in our sample tended to have such relationships between teachers and pupils in the classrooms, between parents and teachers, and between schools and homes. These also tended to be the small schools, as pointed out in Chapter 4. These data remind one of Putnam's regarding the horizontal relationships that characterize his conception of democratic civil communities.

In Chapter 4, I stated that the schools with the most satisfying human connections—which I am now connecting with social democracy—achieved and maintained them without political prodding. Indeed, I even implied that achieving a kind of peace—better stated, perhaps, as an armistice—with reform initiatives was a corollary condition of their success. Would they have been helped in creating environments of the kind I have described, high ranked for satisfaction by teachers and both students and their parents, and which I am now associating with democracy, if the outcome articulated by the entire surround were the development of democratic character?

We are once more caught by the heel—an Achilles' heel—of democracy's character. When does promotion of democracy, particularly in the government arena, approach its being mandated? Do we shortchange our commitment to democracy when we push to high levels of visibility outcomes for schooling that sacrifice the public to the private purpose of schooling, making of education an instrument to ends granted higher value? Since we will have schools and classrooms for quite some time, for the custodial functions and academic outcomes they serve, why not set for them boldly and unequivocally the outcome of democratic character, which they pursue now only if so inclined? That would still leave us free to debate the worth of whatever else we might set for them to do.

For the 3 weeks in the early 1980s that several of us visited one or two elementary and secondary schools almost every day as guests of the People's Republic of China, we went through the same routine each day. Before visiting a classroom, we listened to and questioned the principal's story about the love of country, family, work, and the like being instilled in each student, the wording of each love and good scarcely varying from school to school. The science and mathematics observed resembled in substance that of schools in the United States and many other countries I have visited except, we thought, for being somewhat more advanced at the upper levels than in the United States. There appeared to be somewhat greater teacher control and dominance and perhaps more didactic teaching. It was difficult to tell whether mathematics was being taught as a closed structure or, as Colin Hannaford recommends (see endnote 28 of this chapter), a personal adventure of intelligence and discipline productive of democratic morality.[36]

We have our own routines and symbols of national allegiance and patriotism observed in schools, at sports events, and at a huge variety of gatherings. They are not sufficient for development of the individual and collective democratic character we celebrate. Forthright commitment to it both outside of and inside schools would provide something resembling the model of Figure 5.3. The description accompanying Figure 4.5 is of mission-driven school renewal with the school an ecosystem responsive to its surround.[37] Figure 5.3 shows the process of renewal guided by democratic mission with the daily outcome that of democratic character.

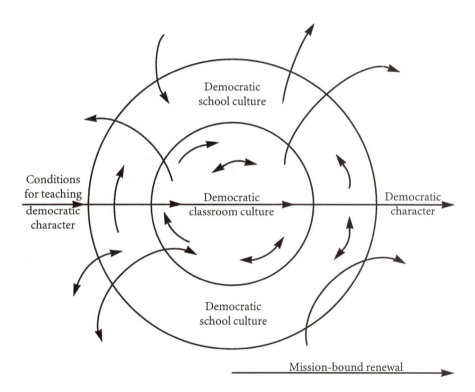

Figure 5.3. A Mission-driven, Responsive, Ecological Model of School Renewal, with Inputs Deliberately Designed for the Development of Democratic Character as Desired, Articulated Outcome

The traditional input-output paradigm probably will be around for as long as we continue to have schools, and so I have deliberately provided an output appropriate for schools required for civil communities—democratic character. I have also designated "conditions for teaching democratic character" the dominant input in support of democratic school and classroom cultures. A major condition is the presence in classrooms of teachers liberally educated and well grounded in the tenets of democracy and caring pedagogy. The intent is to envision a model that aligns expectations for schools on the outside with life on the inside and provides schools with what they need for the realization of these expectations. It pains me somewhat to seek to blend into Figure 5.3 the paradigm of school reform that has created so much dissonance for schools. However, since this is the model of so many people who have the well-being of schools in mind, perhaps the effort to direct it to moral purpose will not be in vain.

Stewardship

The intent of Figure 5.3 is to suggest congruence among our expectations for schools—both formally articulated as outcomes and implicit in the community—the climate and regularities of the schools, and the ambience and practices of the classrooms. For the classroom box of Figure 5.2, I substituted in Figure 5.3 a circle to suggest resonance rather than dissonance with the school surround. For example, implementation of the moral principle regarding the school's readiness for all children is built into the daily practices of all classrooms. I also removed the linear paradigm of teachers "working on" students to produce outcomes (T——> S ——> O). The dominance of this model is revealed in data showing that teacher-to-student talk exceeds all other talk in the teaching and learning classroom relationship by a ratio of at least 2 to 1. The intent is to suggest conversation in which everyone is a participant and learner.

Is it reasonable to assume a working consensus among the people of a democratic society regarding the need for such schools? Is it reasonable to assume the provision of a public system of such schools as a civic responsibility? Is it reasonable to assume the assurance of equal access to these schools and to common provision in them of the education developing democratic character requires? What arguments can be legitimately mounted to counter these assumptions in a democratic society?

Only one argument—that pertaining to freedom to choose not to participate—appears possible. But this smacks of being a self-defeating freedom. Recall the case of the Italian village (Chapter 3) where there was no association beyond the individual family—a situation Banfield classified as amoral familism. A democratic society requires participation. But it is difficult to conceive of a civilization where nobody withdraws. The question arises as to how large this percentage can be without endangering the health of the society.

Our society appears to have a consensus on the need to tax ourselves (with the granting of some exceptions) to sustain an infrastructure that includes roads, parks, water, and an array of public offices and services to meet our individual and collective needs. Some Goodlad family tax dollars are in the roads and parks of Seattle. But no section of these parks and roads is marked for our private use. There is a Goodlad Street in Burnaby, British Columbia, an artifact of property purchased before and lost during the Great Depression of the 1930s. This identification provides no special privileges with respect to observing the street's speed limit; nor does it absolve me of responsibility for observing the traffic light that controls a busy intersection. Yet, I know that Goodlad tax dollars once helped clear the dirt road on which the paved one now rests.

Why should these rules of payment and use for an infrastructure most people want but some people do not use not apply to something as important to our democratic infrastructure as schools? The decade of the 1990s rippled with dissonance over the right to take back from the public tax coffers in the form of vouchers an amount just short of the per pupil cost of schooling to create or seek out a school that aligns with private purpose. Our society seems to have gotten along quite well on the principle that it is all right for some people to have their own private parks, pools, and putting greens in their backyards and even schools in their homes so long as they do not withdraw from the public till the funds voted by a majority of the people to provide such for everyone. But even in the exercise of such freedoms, the state places some controls thought necessary for the common good. Teaching the young apparently is widely considered to be sufficiently risk-laden to warrant certain controls with respect to the freedom to home-school. I worry a bit about the looseness of these controls when the father in a home-schooling family responds to a telephone effort to contact his wife, "Nope, she ain't here."

In our democracy we dare not run the risk of omitting from the infrastructure a well-supported system of public schooling commonly committed to the development of democratic character during the critical passage of our young people from childhood to adulthood. In effect, commitment to and stewardship of such a system is a moral imperative of civic responsibility. Major issues surround the imperative of stewardship. We are not required to use the public services our tax dollars provide, but, if we do, there are rules and regulations to observe and penalties for their nonobservance. To what extent should these conditions embrace our public system of schooling?

There appear to be some contradictions in the provision and use of public schools. On one hand, we have a long history of a sense of need for schools to enculturate the young into the meaning and responsibilities of citizenship, a need heightened by the diverse characteristics of immigrants. However, a significant segment of the population advocates the removal of students perceived to be deterring the progress of others. Suspension of those who seriously disturb the school and classroom environments has been a common practice for generations. But we also spend significant money and time on seeking out truants and keeping them in school. There are subtleties in the dissonance between compulsory attendance and school requirements challenged as interfering with individual freedom (dress codes, for example).

The public purpose of schooling in a democracy appears to bring with it two basic conditions. First, there needs to be a *compulsory system* of public schooling, for all the reasons put forward in this and preceding chapters. That is, the maintenance of such a system is a civic requirement. Second, there should be clear, enforceable agreements regarding the responsibilities of both schools and patrons—a kind of compact. Spelling out the principles and details of such a compact is a task requiring an approach similar to that of hammering out the nation's Constitution.

On the school side of this compact lies clarification of mission: enculturation of the young into our social and political democracy; providing access to a knowledge-rich journey of self-transcendence. On the patron side is responsibility for observing in the use of the school the civilities necessary to its effective functioning. Within the civic framework of these mutual responsibilities, it would be appropriate and probably necessary for each school setting to work out collaboratively its own set of specific agreements.

Prior to the opening of Hawthorne Elementary School in Seattle, Washington, the designated principal, John Morefield, was charged with developing its mission. He consulted widely, beginning with the assumption that a school designed especially to serve poor children of color would readily serve *all children*. One of his basic assumptions would rise naturally as a local interpretation of a nationwide commitment to the public purpose of schooling: "If we are going to change the dominant cultural value system from competition and rugged individualism to cooperation and relationship, it means that we must put forth the behavior that recognizes that human beings need warmth, love, affection, and affirmation. And that children learn and thrive in that nurturing kind of an environment."[38]

Seattle is a city of controlled public school choice, endeavoring to honor the first or second parental choice. Unlike private schools, however, the individual Seattle public schools do not have authority to choose their students from those to whom the district has granted admission. At Hawthorne, there is a supplemental choice. Parent or guardian may choose to sign the *Academic Achievement Warranty* detailing mutual commitments of parent and school (signed by the principal). This is shown in Figure 5.4

At the time of this writing, there is much talk and political activity regarding schools of choice, most of it argued from the perspective of parents' rights and schools' accountability. If such schools are to serve their public democratic purpose, there must be recognition by parents of their responsibilities to the schools they choose.

Concluding Comments on Educational Conditions

Of the many issues that arise out of individual and collective responsibility for a compulsory system of schooling, two policy issues deserve serious attention. The first is whether use of the system by and for children of a specified age range should be compulsory. The second is whether a federal department of education is the appropriate vehicle for monitoring attention to both the public purpose of a system of schooling and the larger educative infrastructure of which this system is a part.

Compulsory Attendance?

As discussed above, there is an internal inconsistency in requiring that young people of an age group attend school and barring

Figure 5.4 The Hawthorne Academic Achievement Warranty

A basic aim of our society is to help each person to fulfill the promise that is within him or her. Schools are a primary means of achieving this goal. In order to achieve this goal, we must recognize that students differ in their abilities, interests and aptitudes and we must provide programs of study to meet these differences. As professional educators, we recognize that individuals differ in their rate of learning and methods by which they learn. We recognize the importance of directed teaching, monitoring, evaluating, reteaching when necessary, and tutoring or coaching as needed.

We offer an Academic Achievement Warranty. Hawthorne School will guarantee that by the end of grade five each student who has been with us since kindergarten will be achieving at grade level or better in reading, mathematics and language arts. In order to provide this guarantee, Hawthorne School will offer early intervention, accelerated instruction, tutorial help and any and all strategies necessary to ensure success.

Various types of assistance will be offered throughout the years— Chapter I assistance, paid tutoring, volunteer tutoring, special education, etc. All instruction and/or tutoring will be geared toward directed teaching and assignments made by the homeroom teacher. The principal will strive for uninterrupted teaching time and teachers will strive for regular daily time on task for reading, mathematics and language arts instruction.

Under this program, parents will agree to the following:

1. Parents agree to keep the student in school at least ninety (90) percent of the time.
2. Parents agree to send the student to school with appropriate classroom supplies.
3. Parents agree to stress reasonable levels of expected behavior for the student. The student will not disrupt the learning environment for himself/herself or his/her classmates.
4. Parents will assist the student with assigned homework and, if necessary, work with the school to arrange for the student to participate in tutoring sessions before, during or after school or on the weekend at no cost to the parents.
5. Parents will agree to attend scheduled conferences. Conferences may be scheduled at the request of the parents or the teacher.

By the cooperative efforts of parents, teachers, administrators and students, we fully believe that the Academic Achievement Warranty can be implemented at Hawthorne School and all children will succeed.

Figure 5.4 *continued*

HAWTHORNE ELEMENTARY SCHOOL
4100 39th Ave. S., Seattle, WA 98118

ACADEMIC ACHIEVEMENT WARRANTY

Student Name

We/I have read the *Academic Achievement Warranty* and agree to do the following:

1. We/I agree to keep the student in school at least ninety (90) percent of the time.
2. We/I agree to send the student to school with appropriate classroom supplies.
3. We/I agree to stress reasonable levels of expected behavior for the student. The student will not disrupt the learning environment for himself/herself or his/her classmates.
4. We/I will assist the student with assigned homework and, if necessary, work with the school to arrange for the student to participate in tutoring sessions before, after or during school or on the weekend at no cost to us/me.
5. We/I will agree to attend scheduled conferences. Conferences may be scheduled at the request of the parent or the teacher.

Parent(s)/Guardian(s) Signature

Principal Signature

Date

them from attendance when they do not. In spite of the effort made to maintain school attendance, a sizeable number of school-age children are at home, on the streets, or in the shopping malls during class sessions. Would attendance figures go up or down if we not only eliminated the compulsory requirement but simultaneously introduced warranties of mutual agreement such as that of Hawthorne? Another condition would be choice in the public domain of schooling, an arrangement that has become increasingly common in recent years. To this we would add electronically delivered instruction to serve those regions, widespread throughout the country, where geography and population limit or remove choice and where, too often, there are not well-qualified teachers in all curricular domains of available schools. Let us then add to these conditions that of redirecting the human and financial resources now devoted to a somewhat primitive effort to keep students in school to support instead the remediation of conditions now making it difficult for some children to attend school.

Given implementation of the above, would school attendance decline or increase? I believe the latter. Given such implementation, would our schools decline or improve in quality? I believe the latter. Would the tearing of the fabric of public schooling by private interest decline? I believe so. Do we have the wisdom to design the whole and the courage to give it a good try? I hope so.

The first negative rejection will be one of cost. In Chapter 4 and elsewhere,[39] I have at least outlined the shape of a redesigned scope of schooling intended to give increased attention to the early years, as well as a different instructional delivery system—both attainable at present cost levels. The question, however, is how much we are willing to pay to ground our democracy in education. What I propose would cost no more but would satisfy us more, whatever the financial commitment we are willing to make.

We can predict, however, that not all young people of school age would be embraced by what I propose. There still will be parents who keep their children out for religious and other reasons, parents who are indifferent, parents who believe they own their children's services for their own adult needs, and young people who defy the wishes of family and community. How large a portion of the citizenry not receiving the socializing benefits of schooling can a democracy afford? My assumption, stated above, is that the out-of-school group will be smaller than what we have today—but this would still be too large. Of particular concern are those children denied school by circumstances not of their own choosing. Do we not have a moral responsibility toward them? I believe we do. This brings us to the issue of national civic responsibility.

A Department of Health, Education, and Welfare?

At the time of this writing, the proposal to abolish the federal department of education is receiving as much or more attention than it did during the early Reagan presidency. I am not among those who favored the initial decision to take education out of the Department of Health, Education, and Welfare. I liked this combination of human-centered service agencies. Also, I preferred that the top official in education—then the Commissioner—continue to be an educator, a condition that was bound to change with designation of a Secretary. I wish that the latter reason entered into those arguments for abolishing the department, but such has not been articulated. The proposal to join it with the Department of Energy not only sounds bizarre but also smacks of the view that education and schooling exist to fuel the needs of commerce and industry.

I have argued in the foregoing for educative communities in which all of our human-centered agencies, including schools, assume responsibility not only for providing services but also for educating everyone in the understandings and abilities they need for taking care of themselves and one another. There will be children who grow unschooled into adolescence and adulthood. Some of these will be disadvantaged because of unfortunate family circumstances more amenable to health and welfare than to school intervention. Some of these will be victims of parental neglect and abuse—the major enviromental sources of children's malfunctioning. Consequently, we must endeavor in every way possible to provide a safety net that includes second chances.

Many adolescents denied opportunity in their childhood, now independent but not empowered, are ready to benefit from community-based formal, informal, and nonformal educational opportunities of the kind suggested in Chapter 3. There must be no academic prerequisites for these. We have gone much too far in designing a school-based rite of passage for entry into an adult world, a rite that would benefit enormously from vitae encompassing abilities extending far beyond the proposed entry certifications of initial academic mastery. Surely the concept of thinking embraces more than thinking for a living[40] and includes multiple intelligences.[41] Human beings are not just the wealth of nations. They are the links in humankind's continuity.

A federal Department of Health, Education, and Welfare—most certainly not a Department of Education and Energy—has the potential for articulating the mission and shaping the agenda of educative communities. If we continue with a Department of Education, however, it must be not only of schools, colleges, and universities but of Education writ large.

CHAPTER 6

Education and the Self

I began Chapter 1 with reference to education as a ubiquitous phenomenon. Educational stimuli of one kind or another surround and shape the self. Indeed, there would be no selfhood absent this surround.

Stirred, prodded, and stimulated by the educative context, the maturing individual engages in a process of self-transcendence from narcissism to identify with and assume responsibility for humankind and for all the species of flora and fauna on which humankind's own survival depends. I closed Chapter 4 with reference to the ecocentric environmental ethic maturity requires and the development of democratic character as the educational journey of self-transcendence.

Because this journey is so endangered by alternatives lushly advertised in travel folders that offer more and earlier self-gratification for less self-discipline and sacrifice, I have endeavored to capitalize in my own arguments on two often-praised attributes of humankind. The first is human fascination with complexity. Part of this is suggested in Robert Rosen's reference (Chapter 5) to self-development's requiring a rich sensory input. Oliver Sacks reports his fascination with the institutionalized twin brothers (formally classified as feeble-minded) who not only performed exceedingly complex mental arithmetic computations but who also took delight in doing so (and in Sacks's inability to keep up).[1] Our too-sharp delineation of learning paths for ourselves and others often crushes out meanings that might be derived. A major function of education is to increase our capacity to see, hear, smell, and contemplate what otherwise would be repetitive and commonplace. A park with trees and grass carefully manicured has sensory appeal but lacks the challenge to the imagination of woods untouched by human hands. What diversity of animal, bird, and plant life flourishes there?

The second attribute is the seeking and satisfaction that arise out of identifying with and imagining about the universe—large and small, close and far, human and nonhuman—that extends beyond whatever sense of personal space we have. We resort to an extraordinary array of avenues, most traveled vicariously, to reach what eludes beyond the precious thoughts and meanings derived. When reason does not quite suffice, faith often takes over. The search for a larger sense of identity—a more multidimensional personhood, if you will—can be fraught with danger. One wonders how much the need to be simultaneously both participant and observer in human drama drove the writer F. Scott Fitzgerald to alcoholism and early death.

It is the role of education in honing these attributes of the self that inspires my praise. And it is the ways in which education is corrupted to lesser ends than guiding the delicate process of self-transcendence that arouses my wrath. The process is massaged and then aborted by voices exhorting the message, "Take now." It requires a whole culture to teach the moral ethic of ensuring that each generation is a good parent to the next.

Part of being a good parent to the next generation is being wise enough not to predict precisely the specific human attributes the well-being of that generation will require. A self-defeating propensity of each generation is to seek to mold tomorrow's adults in the image of today's. The process is one of seeking to inhibit certain tendencies in the young, not because they are evil but because they threaten the beliefs of parents, teachers, and other adults. The result is a narrowing of the educative context that might well impoverish the array of talent available to the next generation. A wise parent generation values and cultivates diversity. Daniel Quinn's conversational gorilla, Ishmael, states the principle this way:

> "Diversity is a survival factor *for the community itself*. A community of a hundred million species can survive almost anything short of total global catastrophe. Within that hundred million will be thousands that could survive a global temperature drop of twenty degrees—which would be a lot more devastating than it sounds. Within that hundred million will be thousands that could survive a global temperature rise of twenty degrees. But a community of a hundred species or a thousand species has almost no survival value at all."[2]

The best assurance of the diversity necessary to survival and, beyond survival, self-fulfilling individual lives is not the careful selection of slots and the matching of individuals to them but the cultivation of diversely talented individuals. This means the articulation of broad, comprehensive, complex goals for education (such as development of democratic character) that nourish the common-weal and latitude for unique, even unpredictable, individuality. The educational challenge is to till and provide nutrients for fields of almost limitless human dreams. The fields are likely to be narrowly furrowed and sparsely planted when the goals are narrow, precise, and lacking in complexity. Selves do aspire to goals. But it is the journeys that inform and fulfill the self. Linear rationality that tightly joins means to ends narrows the scope of imagination and creativity.

The Compleat Angler

In Chapter 5, I quoted a statement regarding an educational journey that seeks out the unique qualities in all things. This is not, however, merely a safari of encyclopedic collecting—the sort of journey so many parents impose on their very young children. In one of our favorite restaurants, my wife and I watched in near-disbelief a mother take her two young daughters through a regimen of assorted facts, a little of naming things in French, and an array of definitions (*ennui* was the special word for the evening). They might as well have been dining on junk food in a deserted skating rink. The process of understanding and savoring the qualities of things is not preparation for a recitation but development of the self.

In Chapter 5, I discussed the mission and the agenda of the National Network for Educational Renewal, an initiative in the simultaneous renewal of schools and the education of educators. At the core is a leadership program for school and university leaders in the member settings who read the same books and papers over the course of a year and come together for 20 days (in four sessions) of intensive conversation. For most of the participants (at least half of whom hold doctorates) this is a unique experience. Instead of a long list of suggested readings, we provide in clusters for each session and require the reading of about a dozen carefully selected books. Even with this concentration of reading and conversation, a frequent request is for even more time focused on certain books. One wonders about the impact on the self of those long lists of assigned but not-discussed readings. Getting into the meanings and enjoying the modes, rhythms, and lilt of the author's prose appears not to be the intent. By contrast, the reading and discussion of a book a week in the graduate seminars of my colleague Donna Kerr appears far more in keeping with the role of education in self-realization.

To be educative, the surround must provide for more than getting there. One must take considerable personal responsibility for this. We too readily blame others for the impoverished nature of our daily context. Another colleague, Roger Soder, assumes that the reader has some responsibility for readying herself or himself for joining a writer's narrative. Coming panting and sweating from the racquetball court may be better followed by checking one's e-mail than by settling down with Homer, Augustine, Tolstoy, McLuhan, Stein, or Rand. To best appreciate Hemingway's *The Old Man and the Sea*, one is well-advised to take it in one sitting, whereas a selection from a collection of fine poetry lends itself well to 15 minutes before bedtime.

And what responsibilities do we have to the expression of our own thoughts, particularly in the sharing of them with others? Russell Baker, columnist of *The New York Times* and current host of Masterpiece Theatre, wrote nostalgically of the days of slowly writing with quill pen. The effect of the medium lent itself well to having something to say and saying it well. E. Annie Proulx, author of the Pulitzer Prize–winning *The Shipping News*, speaks of the aesthetics of shaping the letters and words of her handwritten manuscripts. Modern technological communications get messages there, but, as Marshall McLuhan pointed out prophetically, the medium so shapes the message that the medium itself becomes the message.[3] In needing to fit the medium, the message is drained of the richness that might captivate the sensibilities and sensitivities of the developing self.

Peter Bodo heralded the year 1993 as the 400th anniversary of the birth of Izaak Walton, author of *The Compleat Angler*. Unlike the array of fishing manuals to be found in most sporting goods stores, with their displays of all manner of gadgets and contrivances for the catching of fish, *The Compleat Angler* celebrates fish, fishing, and the natural context in which fisherfolk fish. Walton lived and wrote by the ethic of naturalist, not predator, an impassioned naturalist who perceived every fish as a marvel of creation among other marvels of creation. Bodo wrote: "The moment I open the volume I can smell the willows and wild roses and hear the songs of the thrassel and blackbird, that so delighted and moved Walton's narrator, Piscator."[4]

Ends and Means Revisited

Bodo's celebration of *The Compleat Angler* takes me back to the conventional linear model of school reform and the alternative ecological model presented in Chapter 4 and revisited in Chapter 5. Our passion for getting there and catching things blinds our vision of what education is and corrupts our conduct of it. The 20th century witnessed in the United States and in other Western countries successive eras of intense infatuation, followed by considerable disillusionment, with variously stated precise outcomes akin to what one finds in training manuals, from fly fishing to weed killing.

Writing in 1918, Franklin Bobbitt virtually dismissed the childhood years as having any value beyond developing abilities that make up the affairs of adult life.[5] Six years later, he went on to list some 821 such abilities (actually many more, since subdivisions ranged from 1 to 20 in number).[6] According to Bobbitt, the precise delineation of these abilities as ends virtually dictated the means. Although he later backed down considerably from this position, virtually to the point of recantation, his texts initiated, according to Philip Jackson, "what was soon to become a burgeoning field of professional activity."[7]

This concept of rational linearity has dominated curricular thought, rising from time to time to a level of acceptance that brings down on alternatives a charge of irrationality. It is fascinating to note both the ahistorical surfacing of the concept in successive eras and the brief periods of disillusionment that seem to serve as prelude to the next ushering in of the old, all dressed up as the new panacea. Those with the first news of the new often are those who later wish to remove any image of their having been early messengers or users.

I find it even more fascinating to note the degree to which there appears to be unawareness of the general dominance of the ends-means linear model so that there is always a welcome mat for it in reform eras, no matter how dressed or bottled. Accompanying this belief, very often, is the notion that a sharpening up of ends will make of education a more efficient instrument, sufficient to offset the dominance of Deweyan theories of self-realization. The question has been raised, "How would our schools be conducted if the work of Edward L. Thorndike had won out over that of John Dewey?" The reference to Dewey's contemporary is directed to Thorndike's contribution to the precise ordering of number combinations such as those of the so-called times tables. One has only to look at the arithmetic texts used over many decades to realize that the assumption of Dewey's dominance is mistaken.

When Rationality Becomes Irrational

It is comforting for contextually oriented curriculum theorists to note the cycle of disaffection replacing enthusiasm for precisely defined ends-means relationships in education with the aging of reform eras and reformers. But this is to ignore the long-term impact of successive eras that take attention away from the educational conditions required for maturation of individual and collective democratic character. I have noted the degree to which the casual, low-status treatment of teacher education has placed well-intentioned, ill-prepared individuals in situations of great responsibility where they must search for appealing ways to substitute for their lack of thorough professional grounding. The rational, linear model carries with it precisely this appeal.

One experience with a group of teachers enamored with the model's rationality and apparent practicality comes to mind. I once observed a staff development session self-conducted by a faculty group gaining high visibility for efficient teaching. One of their number, frequently involved in consulting in schools elsewhere, was conducting an exercise in teaching children kickball. He began with justification of the activity based on one of seven cardinal principles of education—preparing for the wise use of leisure time now and in the future. My first thought was one of wondering about accuracy in predicting the future usefulness of something quite precise learned now. This brought me back to wondering whose wisdom placed kickball in the category of wise use of leisure time now. This progression or regression got me thinking about transfer and the possibility that the learning of kickball is extensively imbued with transfer values. Remembering the realization that my own school experience with group sports (because there were no financial resources for the teaching of individual sports), which I richly enjoyed, left me with only spectator skills as an adult, simply because adulthood for most of us does not come with readily assembled teams of 5, 9, or 11. I developed no repertoire of golf, tennis, sailing, or skiing. I became increasingly uncomfortable with the philosophical justification of kickball.

By now, the session had advanced to technique—a precise series of steps to be taught that, if followed, would make of the learner a competent kickballer. The lesson ended quite suddenly with a precise summing up, from justification to the requirements of mastery. Any questions? There were none, save mine. Mine were of my reflections. Why kickball today for adulthood tomorrow? Why the teaching of precise steps prior to play? Why not a brief introduction of the game, followed by a carefully observed period of play designed to single out necessary skills already acquired? Why not . . . ?

At first the group was puzzled. They knew me as an educator of some modest reputation. How could I be so stupid (conveyed but not directly spoken) as not to understand something so patently obvious? Then, as they began to understand that I understood but had reservations, puzzlement turned to a mixture of disappointment and hostility. One of the most hostile knew of my leisure time enjoyment of fishing and suggested we use this rather than kickball as the unit of selection.

I said something to the effect that I would prefer for the group to leave my fishing alone, but they so jumped on this obviously perfect opportunity to simultaneously justify and edify that I reluctantly gave in to what I sensed would be a greater contretemps than the one already evoked. And so, to the fishing grounds we embarked. But the group was so outcome-certain and clear and so outcome-aligned that we did not get away from the dock.

There was no need to justify fishing as worthy use of my leisure time, presumably, because it already was. What was needed was to operationalize the vague goal of fishing into something more specifically behavioral: to catch fish—specifically, in my case, salmon. But, I said, this would be irrational. For how long do humans perseverate in behavior that appears not to produce the stated outcome, especially if it is clearly stated, without raising essentially moral questions about end, means, or both?

This puzzled the group until I explained that, once upon a time, I usually came home with a salmon but, for some years, I often come home without one. Further, I usually was in company with other boats, sometimes more than a few, and frequently perceived that no salmon were boarded on those boats either. Obviously, to be rational, it was time to quit fishing. Yet, time after time, after answering in the negative my wife's question about catching a fish, I rhapsodized on the pleasures of my day: the pod of orca whales that moved through the fishing ground, undoubtedly feeding on any fish that also happened along; the wonderful conversations of the diving birds as they surfaced one after the other; the bald eagle sitting on a tree stump, solemnly watching us pass by; the warm, late afternoon sun on my back most of the way home. Yes, something would have been added were tomorrow's salmon dinner securely confined in the cockpit's fish box. Of course, to be rational and efficient in the expenditure of time and money, I should fish only when I have learned that schools of salmon are passing through, only on the tides the experts have decreed most likely, and only in the swirling riffs and riffles where some salmon, sometimes, are most prone to strike some lures. But, oh, I would miss so much of what I go fishing for.

I do not know how much our conversation "took." I do know that it created confusion and frustration, both of which are often crucibles for learning and revisiting what one believes already learned. I know that at least several of these fine people came to realize that, for me, going fishing is merely a placeholder for a bouquet of experiences that bring me satisfaction, enjoyment, and insights that I find not only meaningful in their own right but useful during the much greater period of time when I am not fishing. In my childhood, small businesses sometimes closed unexpectedly, leaving on the front door the sign GONE FISHING. It is a joy to imagine the many different wonders disguised by what appears to be such an obvious message.

Gone Fishing: On the Compleat Pursuit of Education

Alan Lightman has written a delightful little book, *Einstein's Dreams*, in which Einstein speculates about the nature of time. A poorly paid patent clerk in his home town of Basel, Switzerland, Einstein dreams about the daily consequences of people looking at time in different ways. We are led through vignettes illustrating the consequences of time moving faster at the center than around the circumference of earth's sphere, moving backward, standing still, and so on. The intellect is challenged and stretched. Then, there are interludes, like the intermissions of play or opera, when we spend time casually with Einstein and his friend Besso—strolling through quiet streets in late afternoon, sitting at noon in an outdoor cafe, and fishing:

> Einstein and Besso sit in a small fishing boat at anchor in the river. Besso is eating a cheese sandwich while Einstein puffs on his pipe and slowly reels in a lure.

"Do you usually catch anything here, smack in the middle of the Aare?" asks Besso, who has never been fishing with Einstein before.

"Never," answers Einstein, who continues to cast.

"Maybe we should move closer to the shore, by those reeds."

"We could," says Einstein. "Never caught anything there, either. You got another sandwich in that bag?"

Besso hands Einstein a sandwich and a beer. He feels slightly guilty for asking his friend to take him along on this Sunday afternoon. Einstein was planning to go fishing alone, in order to think.

"Eat," says Besso. "You need a break from pulling in all those fish."[8]

It has been said by persons who took classes from John Dewey that he often appeared to be elsewhere. As he lectured, he tended to look over and beyond the students and, sometimes, out of the windows to buildings beyond. Quite frequently, on ending, he said, "Thank you, ladies and gentlemen, I think I am a little clearer on these matters now."

Thank you, reader. I think I am a little clearer on some things now. The time is come once more to go fishing.

Notes

Chapter 1

1. Vandenberg, *Education as a Human Right: A Theory of Curriculum and Pedagogy*, p. 3.
2. Greene, *The Dialectic of Freedom*, p. 23.
3. Pusey, *The Age of the Scholar*.
4. Bradbury, *Fahrenheit 451*.
5. Dewey, *Democracy and Education*.
6. Habermas, *Theory and Practice*.
7. Bellah et al., *The Good Society*.
8. For a critique of one of the most comprehensive and carefully grounded utopian conceptions (namely, B. F. Skinner, *Walden Two*), see Sarason, *The Creation of Settings and the Future Societies*, chap. 12.
9. Undoubtedly, some readers will object to my concentration on the mind as the focus of the educational process and will ask, "But what about the heart?" My position is that such qualities as compassion and integrity are of the mind, a mind fine-tuned to what it means to be human. When we speak about matters "of the heart," we are reaffirming the importance of the capacity of the mind to go far beyond synapses of logical meaning to synapses of sensitive feeling. In thinking of "mind," I am referring to the millions of synapses that transcend the programmable neural connections of the brain in their complexity. Education has to do with the whole of this complexity and its infinite possibilities. For further discussion, see Edelman, *Bright Air, Brilliant Fire: On the Matter of the Mind*.
10. National Commission on Excellence in Education, *A Nation at Risk*.
11. Bull, "The Limits of Teacher Professionalization," p. 91.
12. See Tyler, "Why Do We Have Public Schools in a Democracy?" p. vii.
13. Hutchins, "The Great Anti-School Campaign," p. 154.
14. Richman, *Separating School and State: How to Liberate America's Families*, p. xi.
15. Kerr, "Authority and Responsibility in Public Schooling," p. 22.
16. Cremin, *American Education: The Colonial Experience, 1607–1783*, p. xiii.

17. Scheffler, "Basic Mathematical Skills: Some Philosophical and Practical Remarks," pp. 205–212.

18. Kerr, "Authority and Responsibility in Public Schooling," p. 23.

19. Fenstermacher, *Where Are We Going? Who Will Lead Us There?*

20. Dewey, "Philosophy and Democracy," p. 44.

21. Goodlad, Soder, and Sirotnik (Eds.), *The Moral Dimensions of Teaching.*

22. White, *Education and the Good Life.*

23. Cremin, *Popular Education and Its Discontents.*

24. Similar practices abound in the business world from which many management practices in schooling have been derived. See, for example, Peters and Waterman, *In Search of Excellence.*

25. Even though much school reform is driven at the outset by the moral intent of making things better, making things more efficient tends to become dominant. For further discussion, in historical perspective, see McMannon, *Morality, Efficiency, and Reform: An Interpretation of the History of American Education.*

26. Sarason, *The Predictable Failure of Educational Reform.*

27. The Nobel Prize–winning economist Theodore W. Schultz noted the near absence of human capital developed through education in the economic growth models that dominated the economic literature of his time. See his *Investment in Human Capital: The Role of Education and of Research.* We appear to be once more in a time of such neglect.

28. Sarason, *Revisiting "The Culture of the School and the Problem of Change".*

29. McNeil, *Contradictions of Control: School Structure and School Knowledge.*

30. Sizer, *High School Reform and the Reform of Teacher Education.*

31. After studying the frequency with which individuals demonstrating a particular competence are promoted to work requiring quite different competencies, Laurence Peter formulated and refined his Peter Principle in *The Peter Principle.*

32. Andrews, *Braeburn Elementary School, 1967–1990: An Innovation That Survived.*

33. Research shows that parents do want schools to be *in loco parentis* for a large part of each day. They want their children to be safe and cared for there. See Goodlad, *A Place Called School,* chap. 3. Recent research reveals that parents perceive attention to this caring custodial function to be missing in school reform. See Johnson and Immerwahr, *First Things First: What Americans Expect From the Public Schools.*

34. For further discussion, see Tarcov, "The Meanings of Democracy," pp. 1–36.

35. Barber, "America Skips School," p. 46.

36. Kerr, "Toward a Democratic Rhetoric of Schooling."

37. Sarason, "And What Is the Public Interest?" pp. 899–905.

38. Quoted in Corn, "Buchanan Rages On: A Potent Trinity—God, Country, and Me," p. 916.

39. Quoted in Corn, "Buchanan Rages On: A Potent Trinity—God, Country, and Me," p. 914.

40. Kerr, "Democracy, Nurturance, and Community," pp. 65–66.

Chapter 2

1. Wirth, "What We Can Learn From Our Experiences With the Deweyan Tradition," p. 5.

2. Barber, *An Aristocracy of Everyone: The Politics of Education and the Future of America*, p. 5.

3. Sarason, "And What Is the Public Interest?" p. 899.

4. For further information and elaboration, see Adler, *We Hold These Truths*.

5. For more discussion, see McCraw, "The Strategic Vision of Alexander Hamilton."

6. Goodlad, "Common Schools for the Common Weal: Reconciling Self-Interest With the Common Good."

7. Oakeshott, *Rationalism in Politics and Other Essays*, p. 364.

8. Oakeshott, *Rationalism in Politics and Other Essays*, p. 9.

9. Oakeshott, *Rationalism in Politics and Other Essays*, p. 367.

10. See Greene, *The Dialectic of Freedom*, particularly chap. 5. This moral community is virtually by definition a caring community; see Noddings, *Caring: A Feminine Approach to Ethics and Moral Education*.

11. Sarason, "And What Is the Public Interest?" p. 904.

12. For further discussion of self-transcendence, see Ulich, *The Human Career: A Philosophy of Self-Transcendence*.

13. Bloom, *Stability and Change in Human Characteristics*.

14. Erikson, *Childhood and Society*, p. 250.

15. Barber, "America Skips School," p. 46.

16. National Governors' Association, *Time for Results*.

17. Barber, *An Aristocracy of Everyone: The Politics of Education and the Future of America*, p. 15.

18. Bull, "The Limits of Teacher Professionalization," p. 92.

19. Bull, "The Limits of Teacher Professionalization," pp. 91–98.

20. Scheffler, "Basic Mathematical Skills: Some Philosophical and Practical Remarks," p. 205.

21. Adler, *We Hold These Truths*, p. 20.

22. Oakeshott, *Rationalism in Politics and Other Essays*, pp. 296–297.

23. This is a modification of the definition put forward by Cremin, *American Education: The Colonial Experience, 1607–1783*, p. xiii: "[Education is] the deliberate, systematic, and sustained effort to transmit or evoke knowledge, attitudes, values, skills, and sensibilities."

24. Gould, *The Mismeasure of Man*, p. 20.

25. Gould, *The Mismeasure of Man*, p. 28.

26. Myrdal, *An American Dilemma: The Negro Problem and Modern Democracy*.

27. Conant, *Slums and Suburbs*.

28. Cited in Gould, *The Mismeasure of Man*, pp. 104–105.

29. Cited in Gould, *The Mismeasure of Man*, pp. 83–84.

30. Cited in Gould, *The Mismeasure of Man*, p. 103.

31. Goodlad, *Teachers for Our Nation's Schools*, chap. 3.

32. See Hilliard, "Misunderstanding and Testing Intelligence."

33. For what I believe to be the most comprehensive treatment in print regarding the American dilemma in seeking to provide all of the people with educational equality, see Miller, *An American Imperative: Accelerating Minority Educational Advancement*.

34. This emerged as a hot topic among post-World War II economists. See Machlup, *Education and Economic Growth*.

35. Schultz, *Investment in Human Capital: The Role of Education and of Research*.

36. Cited by Bradsher, "America's Opportunity Gap," p. E4.

37. Phenix, "Education and the Concept of Man," *Views and Ideas on Mankind*, p. 10.

38. Wagar, *The City of Man: Prophecies of a World Civilization in Twentieth-Century Thought*, p. 163.

39. Wagar, "Religion, Ideology, and the Idea of Mankind in Contemporary History," p. 197.

40. Sarason, "And What Is the Public Interest?" p. 899.

41. Barber, "America Skips School," p. 42.

42. Sarason, "American Psychology, and the Needs for Transcendence and Community," p. 193.

43. Sarason, "American Psychology, and the Needs for Transcendence and Community," p. 193.

44. Tocqueville, *Democracy in America*, p. 536.

45. Tocqueville, *Democracy in America*, p. 534.

46. Barber, "Searching for Civil Society," p. 114.

47. Strauss, *The Political Philosophy of Hobbes: Its Basis and Its Genesis*.

48. Fenstermacher, *Where Are We Going? Who Will Lead Us There?*

49. Goodlad, Soder, and Sirotnik (eds.), *The Moral Dimensions of Teaching*.

50. White, *Education and the Good Life*.

51. Wagar, *The City of Man: Prophecies of a World Civilization in Twentieth-Century Thought*, pp. 171–172.

52. Stapledon, *Last and First Men*, pp. 17–18.

Chapter 3

1. Putnam, "Bowling Alone: America's Declining Social Capital." Putnam's paper prompted much commentary, discussion, and some dis-

agreement. See, for example, Ladd, "The Data Just Don't Show Erosion of America's 'Social Capital.'"

2. Bennett, *The Book of Virtues: A Treasury of Great Moral Stories.*

3. Althusius, *Politica*, p. 17.

4. Althusius, *Politica*, p. 30.

5. Althusius, *Politica*, p. 37.

6. Althusius, *Politica*, p. 43.

7. Althusius, *Politica*, p. 17.

8. Bellah, Madsen, Sullivan, Swidler, and Tipton, *Habits of the Heart: Individualism and Commitment in American Life*, p. 115.

9. Parker (Ed.), *Educating the Democratic Mind*, p. 8.

10. Banfield, *The Moral Basis of a Backward Society*, pp. 83–86.

11. Putnam, *Making Democracy Work: Civic Traditions in Modern Italy*, p. 130.

12. Putnam, *Making Democracy Work: Civic Traditions in Modern Italy*, p. 97.

13. Putnam, *Making Democracy Work: Civic Traditions in Modern Italy*, p. 74.

14. Viviano, "The Fall of Rome," pp. 37–40.

15. Loh, "America: A Nation of Nations," p. E3.

16. van der Post, *A Far-Off Place*, p. 110.

17. Fenstermacher, *The Absence of Democratic and Educational Ideals From Contemporary Educational Reform Initiatives*, pp. 1–2.

18. Fenstermacher, "On Restoring Public and Private Life." Quoted from the original unrevised draft; does not appear in the published version.

19. Bloom, *Stability and Change in Human Characteristics.*

20. Kerr, "Toward a Democratic Rhetoric of Schooling."

21. Elkind, "School and Family in the Postmodern World," p. 13.

22. Ulich, "The Ambiguities in the Great Movements of Thought."

23. Coleman, "Changes in the Family and Implications for the Common School"; *Schools, Families, and Children*; and *Foundations of Social Theory.*

24. Goodlad, "Beyond Half an Education."

25. *Procedural republic* is the terminology of Michael J. Sandel. See Sandel, "The Procedural Republic and the Unencumbered Self."

26. Analyses of elementary school textbooks and courses of study commonly used in schools of the 19th and early 20th century reveal frequent reference to the goal of character development. In their history of the school superintendency, Tyack and Hansot portray school district leaders as "managers of virtue." See Tyack and Hansot, *Managers of Virtue: Public School Leadership in America, 1820–1980.*

27. Green, *Predicting the Behavior of the Educational System.*

28. Frankel, "Scapegoating the Poor," p. E1.

29. Gans, *The War Against the Poor*, p. 115.

30. Cremin, *Popular Education and Its Discontents*, p. 17.

31. Barber, "Searching for Civil Society," p. 114.

32. For documentation, see Goodlad and Keating (Eds.), *Access to Knowledge: An Agenda for Our Nation's Schools.*

33. See, for example, Westbrook, *John Dewey and American Democracy*; and Ryan, *John Dewey and the High Tide of American Liberalism*.

34. Westbrook, "Public Schooling and American Democracy."

35. Dewey, *Democracy and Education*. See especially chap. 7, "The Democratic Conception of Education."

36. Dewey, *Lectures on Psychological and Political Ethics: 1898*, p. 445.

37. Bellah et al., *The Good Society*.

38. Bennett, *The Moral Compass*, p. 12.

39. Greer and Kohl, *A Call to Character*.

40. Parker (Ed.), *Educating the Democratic Mind*.

41. See, for example, Goodlad, *Toward Educative Communities and Tomorrow's Teachers* and *Educational Renewal: Better Teachers, Better Schools*, chap. 7.

42. I acknowledge here my debt to Hal A. Lawson for this notion of a common professional denominator of knowledge, sensitivities, commitments, values, and skills, in his "Expanding the Goodlad Agenda: Interprofessional Education and Community Collaboration in Service of Vulnerable Children, Youth, and Families."

43. Lawson, "Schools and Educational Communities in a New Vision for Child Welfare."

44. Dewey, *The Child and the Curriculum and The Child and Society*, p. 28. (*The Child and the Curriculum* was first published by the University of Chicago Press in 1902.)

45. Bruner, *The Process of Education*.

46. Carroll, "A Model of School Learning."

47. For an explication of these three systems, see La Belle, "Alternative Educational Strategies: The Integration of Learning Systems in the Community."

48. Bill Gates has comprehensively described the medium, peering a little into the human implications of its message, in *The Road Ahead*.

49. Task Force on Early Childhood Education, *Early Childhood Education*.

50. See, for example, Kerr, *Beyond Education: In Search of Nurture*.

51. See, for example, Noddings, *The Challenge to Care in Schools: An Alternative Approach to Education*.

52. Martin, *The Schoolhome*.

53. For a comprehensive review of the nongraded school movement in the second half of the 20th century and a broad array of related concepts coming from research and inquiry, see Anderson and Pavan, *Nongradedness: Helping It To Happen*.

54. Goodlad, *A Place Called School*.

55. This connection is well made by Brosio, *A Radical Democratic Critique of Capitalist Education*, pp. 273–274, 278–292.

56. See Bettelheim, *Children of the Dream*; and Feshback, Goodlad, and Lombard, *Early Schooling in England and Israel*.

57. For a brief account of events before and during the 1957 to 1967

decade of reform intended to make schools more relevant to all students, see Goodlad, "Schooling and Education."

58. School boards all across the United States adopted and charged their district superintendents to implement the comprehensive school concept recommended in 1959 by the highly influential Conant, *The American High School Today*. Conant's recommendations included a differentiated, more demanding curriculum emphasizing more mathematics and science for the college bound, and more vocational-oriented provisions for those enrolled who clearly were not destined for higher education.

59. Miller, *An American Imperative: Accelerating Minority Educational Advancement*.

60. Carnegie Council on Adolescent Development, *Great Transitions: Preparing Adolescents for a New Century*.

61. William T. Grant Foundation Commission on Work, Family and Community, *The Forgotten Half: Pathways to Success for America's Youth and Young Families*.

62. Carnegie Council on Adolescent Development, *Great Transitions: Preparing Adolescents for a New Century*, p. 12.

63. Education and Human Services Consortium, *What It Takes: Structuring Interagency Partnerships to Connect Children and Families With Comprehensive Services*.

64. Bugnion, *Overhauling American Education—The Swiss Way*, unpublished book manuscript made available to this writer in July 1991.

Chapter 4

1. Seymour Sarason popularized the word "regularities" in describing regulatory characteristics common to elementary and secondary schools. See Sarason, *Revisiting "The Culture of the School and the Problem of Change."*

2. McNeil, *Contradictions of Control: School Structure and School Knowledge*.

3. Goodlad, *A Place Called School*.

4. Ryan, *John Dewey and the High Tide of American Liberalism*, p. 340.

5. A rash of books in these years joined Dewey's name with much that the authors perceived to have gone wrong with the schools. Some of these represented a continuation of Dewey's feud with Catholic intellectuals and Robert Maynard Hutchins, president of the University of Chicago. See Bell, *Crisis in Education*; Smith, *And Madly Teach*; Lynd, *Quackery in the Public Schools*; Bestor, *Educational Wastelands*; and Hutchins, *The Conflict in Education in a Democratic Society*.

6. Flesch, *Why Johnny Can't Read*.

7. Hulburd, *This Happened in Pasadena*.

8. For more detailed information regarding the attack on progres-

sive education, particularly that of Arthur Bestor, see Bracey, *Final Exam: A Study of the Perpetual Scrutiny of American Education*, pp. 39–44.

9. Eliot, "Modern Education and the Classics," p. 452.

10. Callahan, *Education and the Cult of Efficiency*.

11. One of the most edifying analyses is that of House, *The Politics of Educational Innovation*.

12. George H. Douglas argues that we have the wrong model of higher education, one that values graduate studies and research to the detriment of undergraduate teaching and liberal learning. See Douglas, *Education Without Impact*.

13. For a history of this shift in selected schools of education in leading universities, see Clifford and Guthrie, *Ed School*.

14. Cartter, "The Cartter Report on the Leading Schools of Education, Law and Business," pp. 44–48.

15. National Commission on Excellence in Education, *A Nation at Risk*.

16. See, for example, the report on a network of formally structured school-university partnerships by Sirotnik and Goodlad (Eds.), *School-University Partnerships: Concepts, Cases, and Concerns*.

17. Goodlad, "On Taking School Reform Seriously."

18. Riley, "If It Looks Like Manure . . .," p. 240.

19. For an analysis of the concept and a comprehensive review of the relevant literature, see Sirotnik, "The School as the Center of Change," in Sergiovanni and Moore (Eds.), *Schooling for Tomorrow: Directing Reform to Issues That Count*. See also Goodlad, *The Dynamics of Educational Change*.

20. For a sensitive, inside look, see Kidder, *Among Schoolchildren*.

21. For a summary of what an insightful student of school reform has learned about effecting change, see Fullan, *Change Forces*.

22. Finn, "The Ho Hum Revolution."

23. An early commentator on this silliness during the second of the two school reform eras described was Kerr, "Is Education Really All That Guilty?"

24. The slogan of the 1986 report of the National Governors' Association, *Time for Results*.

25. Westbrook, "Public Schooling and American Democracy," p. 135.

26. Boyer, *High School*; Goodlad, *A Place Called School*; Sizer, *Horace's School*.

27. Lightfoot, *The Good High School*.

28. See, for example, Hill, *Reinventing Public Education*.

29. McMannon, *Morality, Efficiency, and Reform: An Interpretation of the History of American Education*, p. 45.

30. Fullan, *Change Forces*, especially chap. 4.

31. Wehlage, Smith, and Lipman, "Restructuring Urban Schools: The New Futures Experience." See also Farcus, *Divided Within, Besieged Without*.

32. For a very comprehensive review of the micropolitics of schools, see Malen, "The Micropolitics of Education: Mapping the Multiple Dimensions of Power Relations in School Politics."

33. Sarason, *The Predictable Failure of Educational Reform*, p. 59.

34. For a comprehensive bibliography and insightful analysis, see Fullan, *The New Meaning of Educational Change*.

35. Among the studies of the RAND Corporation supporting this conclusion, one of the most emphatic and definitive is that of Averch et al., *How Effective Is Schooling?*

36. Jackson, *Life in Classrooms*.

37. Sarason, *Revisiting "The Culture of the School and the Problem of Change."*

38. National Board for Professional Teaching Standards, *Toward High and Rigorous Standards for the Teaching Profession*.

39. For an intriguing retrospective on school reform, 1960 to 1990, see Gibboney, *The Stone Trumpet*.

40. Regarding characteristics of this renewing process and differences among the schools regarding them, see Heckman, *Exploring the Concept of School Renewal: Cultural Differences and Similarities Between More or Less Renewing Schools*.

41. Brosio has analyzed the data presented in my *A Place Called School* to establish connections between the practices for organization, teaching, and learning described and basic principles of democracy such as equity. The gulf he presents is highly disturbing. See Brosio, *A Radical Democratic Critique of Capitalist Education*, especially chap. 7.

42. Pomfret, Letter to the Editor, p. A7.

43. For a comprehensive review of research on correlates of school size, see Plecki, *The Relationship Between Middle School Size and Student Achievement* and *The Relationship of Elementary School Size and Student Achievement in California Public Schools*.

44. Goodlad, "An Ecocentric Environmental Ethic as a Foundation for Schooling, Character, and Democracy."

Chapter 5

1. Eco, *The Name of the Rose*, p. 393. Adso, Eco's chronicler of events in an early 14th-century Italian abbey, writes of growing old and recognizing only faith: "The older I grow . . . the less I value intelligence that wants to know and will that wants to do."

2. Vandenberg, *Education as a Human Right: A Theory of Curriculum and Pedagogy*, p. 93.

3. Vandenberg, *Education as a Human Right: A Theory of Curriculum and Pedagogy*, p. 93.

4. Vandenberg, *Education as a Human Right: A Theory of Curriculum and Pedagogy*, p. 92.

5. Feinberg, "The Moral Responsibility of Public Schools."

6. Barber, "Searching for Civil Society."

7. Vandenberg, *Education as a Human Right: A Theory of Curriculum and Pedagogy*, p. 92.

8. Barber, *An Aristocracy of Everyone: The Politics of Education and the Future of America*, p. 7.

9. Ariès, *Centuries of Childhood*, p. 412.

10. Ariès, *Centuries of Childhood*, p. 413.

11. Goodlad, "Common Schools for the Common Weal: Reconciling Self-Interest With the Common Good."

12. McMannon, *Morality, Efficiency, and Reform: An Interpretation of the History of American Education*. See particularly pp. 20–22.

13. Kaestle (Ed.), *Joseph Lancaster and the Monitorial School Movement: A Documentary History*.

14. Simpson, *The Working Man's Manual*, p. 1054.

15. Simpson, *The Working Man's Manual*, p. 1055.

16. Commons et al. (Eds.), *A Documentary History of American Industrial Society*, p. 1059.

17. Sizer, "The Meanings of 'Public Education.'"

18. Darling-Hammond, "Education, Equity, and the Right to Learn."

19. Oakes, *Keeping Track: How Schools Structure Inequality*.

20. Smith and Noble, "Toward a Comprehensive Program of Evaluation," p. 160.

21. *Brown v. Board of Education*.

22. Underwood, "School Finance Adequacy as Vertical Equity."

23. Conant, *Slums and Suburbs*.

24. Miller, "Editorial: Education in a Declining Culture," p. 2.

25. Mathews, *Is There a Public for Public Schools?*, p. 64.

26. Bateson, "Democracy, Ecology, and Participation." See particularly pp. 79–83.

27. See Goodlad, *Teachers for Our Nation's Schools*. The 19 conditions, formulated as postulates, were revised slightly for purposes of clarification in Goodlad, *Educational Renewal: Better Teachers, Better Schools*.

28. The Institute of Democracy From Mathematics (Oxford, England), directed by Colin Hannaford, is committed to advancing the connection between the subject-specific pedagogy of mathematics and democracy. See Goodlad, "Schooling U.S.A.," p. 287.

29. Teilhard de Chardin, *The Phenomenon of Man*.

30. Rosen, "Do We Really Need Ends to Justify the Means?" p. 29.

31. Progress through 1994 is described in Goodlad, "The National Network for Educational Renewal" and "Genesis and Maturation of an Initiative in Educational Renewal: A Janus Look." For a report from many of the NNER settings on their experiences with the development of partner schools, see Osguthorpe, Harris, Harris, and Black (Eds.), *Partner Schools: Centers for Educational Renewal*.

32. Our extensive research into the sources of what teachers in a large sample were teaching placed these three at the top of the list. See Klein, *Teacher Perceived Sources of Influence on What Is Taught in Subject Areas*.

33. Goodlad, *A Place Called School*, pp. 132–136.

34. Coleman, *Equality of Educational Opportunity*.

35. Coleman's response to my query (on a public platform we shared) regarding these factors was that he planned to bring together some statisticians to look into them.

36. For further description of the precepts required to be instilled in each school and the classroom practices observed, see Goodlad and Berris (Eds.), *Report of the Education Foundation Delegation to China, 1981*.

37. For a comprehensive review of growing understanding of and increased use of ecological models and metaphors of schooling, see Sirotnik, "Ecological Images of Change: Limits and Possibilities."

38. Morefield, *Recreating Schools for All Children*, a position paper resulting from Morefield's inquiries and reflections on them, made available to patrons of Hawthorne Elementary School and interested others.

39. Goodlad, *A Place Called School*, chap. 10; *Educational Renewal: Better Teachers, Better Schools*, chap. 7.

40. Marshall and Tucker, *Thinking for a Living: Education and the Wealth of Nations*.

41. Gardner, *Frames of Mind: The Theory of Multiple Intelligences* and *Multiple Intelligences: The Theory in Practice*.

Chapter 6

1. Sacks, *The Man Who Mistook His Wife for a Hat*, pp. 195–213. Sacks describes the twins as hearing "the world symphony . . . but entirely in the form of numbers. The soul is 'harmonical' whatever one's IQ and for some, like physical scientists and mathematicians, the sense of harmony, perhaps, is chiefly intellectual. And yet I cannot think of anything intellectual that is not, in some way, also sensible—indeed the very word 'sense' always has this double connotation. Sensible, and in some sense 'personal' as well, for one cannot feel anything, find anything 'sensible,' unless it is, in some way, related or relatable to oneself" (p. 203).

2. Quinn, *Ishmael*, p. 130.

3. Some of McLuhan's most provocative ideas, many of them remarkably prescient, are contained in Molinaro, McLuhan, and Toye, *Letters of Marshall McLuhan*.

4. Bodo, "On the Compleat Pursuit of Angling, Not Catching," p. 12E.

5. Bobbitt, *The Curriculum*.

6. Bobbitt, *How to Make a Curriculum*.

7. Jackson, "Conceptions of Curriculum and Curriculum Specialists," p. 7. Jackson's thoughtful, balanced piece on curriculum perspectives is well worth a careful reading (pp. 3–40).

8. Lightman, *Einstein's Dreams*, pp. 145–146.

References

Adler, Mortimer J. (1987). *We hold these truths*. New York: Macmillan.

Althusius, Johannes. (1995). *Politica* (F. S. Carney, Ed. & Trans.). Indianapolis, IN: Liberty Press. (Original work published 1603 & 1614)

Anderson, Robert H., & Pavan, Barbara Nelson. (1993). *Nongradedness: Helping it to happen*. Lancaster, PA: Technomics.

Andrews, Jill Brandenfels. (1993). *Braeburn elementary school, 1967–1990: An innovation that survived*. Unpublished doctoral dissertation, University of Washington, Seattle.

Ariès, Phillipe. (1962). *Centuries of childhood* (R. Baldick, Trans.). New York: Vintage Books.

Averch, Harvey A., et al. (1974). *How effective is schooling?* Englewood Cliffs, NJ: Educational Technology Publications.

Banfield, Edward C. (1958). *The moral basis of a backward society*. New York: Free Press.

Barber, Benjamin R. (1992). *An aristocracy of everyone: The politics of education and the future of America*. New York: Ballantine.

Barber, Benjamin R. (1993, November). America skips school. *Harper's Magazine, 286*, 39–46.

Barber, Benjamin R. (1995, Spring). Searching for civil society. *National Civic Review, 84*, 114–118.

Bateson, Mary Catherine. (1996). Democracy, ecology, and participation. In R. Soder (Ed.), *Democracy, education, and the schools* (pp. 69–86). San Francisco: Jossey-Bass.

Bell, Bernard Iddings. (1949). *Crisis in education*. New York: Whittlesey House.

Bellah, Robert N., Madsen, Richard, Sullivan, William M., Swidler, Ann, & Tipton, Steven M. (1985). *Habits of the heart: Individualism and commitment in American life*. Berkeley: University of California Press.

Bellah, Robert N., et al. (1991). *The good society*. New York: Knopf.

Bennett, William J. (1993). *The book of virtues: A treasury of great moral stories*. New York: Simon & Schuster.

Bennett, William J. (1995). *The moral compass*. New York: Simon & Schuster.

Bestor, Arthur E. (1953). *Educational wastelands*. Urbana: University of Illinois Press.

169

Bettelheim, Bruno. (1969). *Children of the dream*. New York: Macmillan.

Bloom, Benjamin S. (1964). *Stability and change in human characteristics*. New York: Wiley.

Bobbitt, Franklin. (1918). *The curriculum*. Cambridge, MA: Riverside Press.

Bobbitt, Franklin. (1924). *How to make a curriculum*. Cambridge, MA: Riverside Press.

Bodo, Pete. (1993, January 3). On the compleat pursuit of angling, not catching. *The New York Times*, p. 12E.

Boyer, Ernest L. (1983). *High school*. New York: Harper & Row.

Bracey, Gerald W. (1995). *Final exam: A study of the perpetual scrutiny of American education*. Bloomington, IN: Technos Press.

Bradbury, Ray. (1953). *Fahrenheit 451*. New York: Ballantine.

Bradsher, Keith. (1995, June 4). America's opportunity gap. *The New York Times*, p. E4.

Brosio, Richard A. (1994). *A radical democratic critique of capitalist education*. New York: Peter Lang.

Brown v. Board of Education. (1954). 347 U.S. 483, 493.

Bruner, Jerome S. (1960). *The process of education*. Cambridge, MA: Harvard University Press.

Bugnion, Jacqueline. (1991). *Overhauling American education—the Swiss way*. Unpublished manuscript.

Bull, Barry L. (1990). The limits of teacher professionalization. In J. I. Goodlad, R. Soder, & K. A. Sirotnik (Eds.), *The moral dimensions of teaching* (pp. 87–129). San Francisco: Jossey-Bass.

Callahan, Raymond E. (1962). *Education and the cult of efficiency*. Chicago: University of Chicago Press.

Carnegie Council on Adolescent Development. (1995). *Great transitions: Preparing adolescents for a new century*. New York: Carnegie Corporation of New York.

Carroll, John B. (1963, May). A model of school learning. *Teachers College Record, 64*, 723–733.

Cartter, Allan. (1977). The Cartter report on the leading schools of education, law and business. *Change, 9*, 44–48.

Clifford, Geraldine J., & Guthrie, James W. (1988). *Ed school*. Chicago: University of Chicago Press.

Coleman, James S. (1966). *Equality of educational opportunity*. Washington, DC: Government Printing Office.

Coleman, James S. (1985). *Schools, families, and children*. 1985 Ryerson Lecture. Chicago: University of Chicago Press.

Coleman, James S. (1990). *Foundations of social theory*. Cambridge, MA: Belknap Press of Harvard University.

Coleman, James S. (1991). Changes in the family and implications for the common school. *University of Chicago Legal Forum*, pp. 153–170.

Commons, John R., et al. (Eds.). (1974). *A documentary history of American industrial society*. Cited in S. Cohen (Ed.), Platform of the Boston Working Man's Party (1830), in *Education in the United States: A documentary history* (p. 1059). New York: Random House.

Conant, James B. (1959). *The American high school today*. New York: McGraw-Hill.

Conant, James B. (1961). *Slums and suburbs*. New York: McGraw-Hill.

Corn, David. (1995). Buchanan rages on: A potent trinity—God, country, and me. *The Nation, 260* (25), 913–916.

Cremin, Lawrence A. (1970). *American education: The colonial experience, 1607–1783*. New York: Harper & Row.

Cremin, Lawrence A. (1990). *Popular education and its discontents*. New York: Harper & Row.

Darling-Hammond, Linda. (in press). Education, equity, and the right to learn. In J. I. Goodlad & T. J. McMannon (Eds.), *The public purpose of education and schooling*. San Francisco: Jossey-Bass.

Dewey, John. (1916). *Democracy and education*. New York: Macmillan.

Dewey, John. (1956). *The child and the curriculum and the child and society*. Chicago: University of Chicago Press. (*The child and the curriculum* originally published 1902)

Dewey, John. (1976). *Lectures on psychological and political ethics: 1898*. New York: Hafner Press.

Dewey, John. (1982). Philosophy and democracy. In J. Boydston (Ed.), *John Dewey: The middle works, 1899–1924: Vol. 11. 1918–1919*. Carbondale: Southern Illinois University Press.

Douglas, George H. (1992). *Education without impact*. New York: Birch Lane Press.

Eco, Umberto. (1983). *The name of the rose* (English trans.). New York: Harcourt Brace Jovanovich.

Edelman, Gerald M. (1992). *Bright air, brilliant fire: On the matter of the mind*. New York: Basic Books.

Education and Human Services Consortium. (1991). *What it takes: Structuring interagency partnerships to connect children and families with comprehensive services*. Washington, DC: Author.

Eliot, T. S. (1950). Modern education and the classics. In *Selected essays*. New York: Harcourt Brace.

Elkind, David. (1995, September). School and family in the postmodern world. *Phi Delta Kappan, 77*, 8–14.

Erikson, Erik H. (1963). *Childhood and society* (2nd ed.). New York: W. W. Norton.

Farcus, Steve (with Johnson, Jean). (1993). *Divided within, besieged without* (Report). New York: Public Agenda Foundation.

Feinberg, Walter. (1990). The moral responsibility of public schools. In J. I. Goodlad, R. Soder, & K. A. Sirotnik (Eds.), *The moral dimensions of teaching* (pp. 155–187). San Francisco: Jossey-Bass.

Fenstermacher, Gary D. (1992, February 25). *Where are we going? Who will lead us there?* Presidential address, American Association of Colleges for Teacher Education annual meeting, San Antonio, TX.

Fenstermacher, Gary D. (1994, June 10). *The absence of democratic and educational ideals from contemporary educational reform initiatives*. Stanley Elam Lecture, Educational Press Association of America, Chicago.

Fenstermacher, Gary D. (in press). On restoring public and private life. In J. I. Goodlad & T. J. McMannon (Eds.), *The public purpose of education and schooling*. San Francisco: Jossey-Bass.

Feshback, Norma D., Goodlad, John I., & Lombard, Avima. (1973). *Early schooling in England and Israel*. New York: McGraw-Hill.

Finn, Chester E., Jr. (1991, Summer). The ho hum revolution. *Wilson Quarterly, 15*, 63–76.

Flesch, Rudolf F. (1955). *Why Johnny can't read*. New York: Harper & Bros.

Frankel, Max. (1995, October 22). Scapegoating the poor. *Seattle Post-Intelligencer*, p. E1. (Copyright 1995 *The New York Times Magazine*)

Fullan, Michael G. (with Stiegelbauer, Suzanne). (1991). *The new meaning of educational change* (2nd ed.). New York: Teachers College Press.

Fullan, Michael. (1993). *Change forces*. New York: Falmer Press.

Gans, Herbert J. (1995). *The war against the poor*. New York: Basic Books.

Gardner, Howard. (1983). *Frames of mind: The theory of multiple intelligences*. New York: Basic Books.

Gardner, Howard. (1993). *Multiple intelligences: The theory in practice*. New York: Basic Books.

Gates, Bill. (1995). *The road ahead*. New York: Viking Penguin.

Gibboney, Richard A. (1994). *The stone trumpet*. Albany: State University of New York Press.

Goodlad, John I. (1969). Schooling and education. In R. M. Hutchins, M. J. Adler, & O. Bird (Eds.), *The great ideas today 1969* (pp. 100–145). Chicago: Encyclopaedia Britannica.

Goodlad, John I. (1975). *The dynamics of educational change*. New York: McGraw-Hill.

Goodlad, John I. (1984). *A place called school*. New York: McGraw-Hill.

Goodlad, John I. (1990). *Teachers for our nation's schools*. San Francisco: Jossey-Bass.

Goodlad, John I. (1992, February 19). Beyond half an education. *Education Week*, pp. 44, 34.

Goodlad, John I. (1992, November). On taking school reform seriously. *Phi Delta Kappan, 74*, 232–238.

Goodlad, John I. (1992). *Toward educative communities and tomorrow's teachers*, Work in Progress Series, No. 1. Seattle, WA: Institute for Educational Inquiry.

Goodlad, John I. (1994). Common schools for the common weal: Reconciling self-interest with the common good. In J. I. Goodlad & P. Keating (Eds.), *Access to knowledge: An agenda for our nation's schools* (2nd ed., pp. 1–21). New York: College Entrance Examination Board.

Goodlad, John I. (1994). *Educational renewal: Better teachers, better schools*. San Francisco: Jossey-Bass.

Goodlad, John I. (1994, April). The National Network for Educational Renewal. *Phi Delta Kappan, 75*, 632–638.

Goodlad, John I. (1995, Spring/Summer). Genesis and maturation of an initiative in educational renewal: A Janus look. *Record in Educational Leadership*, *15*, 3–11.

Goodlad, John I. (1995). Schooling U.S.A. In I. M. Carl (Ed.), *Prospects for school mathematics* (pp. 275–289). Reston, VA: The National Council of Teachers of Mathematics.

Goodlad, John I., & Berris, Jan Carol (Eds.). (1985). *Report of the education foundation delegation to China, 1981*. New York: National Committee on United States-China Relations.

Goodlad, John I., & Keating, Pamela (Eds.). (1994). *Access to knowledge: An agenda for our nation's schools* (2nd ed.). New York: College Entrance Examination Board.

Goodlad, John I., Soder, Roger, & Sirotnik, Kenneth A. (Eds.). (1990). *The moral dimensions of teaching*. San Francisco: Jossey-Bass.

Goodlad, Stephen J. (1996). *An ecocentric environmental ethic as a foundation for schooling, character, and democracy*. Work in progress.

Gould, Stephen J. (1981). *The mismeasure of man*. New York: W. W. Norton.

Green, Thomas F. (1980). *Predicting the behavior of the educational system*. Syracuse, NY: Syracuse University Press.

Greene, Maxine. (1988). *The dialectic of freedom*. New York: Teachers College Press.

Greer, Colin, & Kohl, Herbert. (1995). *A call to character*. New York: HarperCollins.

Habermas, Jürgen. (1974). *Theory and practice*. London: Heinemann Educational Books.

Heckman, Paul E. (1984). *Exploring the concept of school renewal: Cultural differences and similarities between more or less renewing schools* (Tech. Rep. No. 33, A Study of Schooling in the United States). Los Angeles: University of California, Graduate School of Education, Laboratory in School and Community Education.

Hill, Paul T. (1995). *Reinventing public education*. Santa Monica, CA: RAND Corporation.

Hilliard, Asa G., III. (1994). Misunderstanding and testing intelligence. In J. I. Goodlad & P. Keating (Eds.), *Access to knowledge: An agenda for our nation's schools* (2nd ed., pp. 145–157). New York: College Entrance Examination Board.

House, Ernest R. (1974). *The politics of educational innovation*. Berkeley, CA: McCutchan.

Hulburd, David. (1951). *This happened in Pasadena*. New York: Macmillan.

Hutchins, Robert M. (1953). *The conflict in education in a democratic society*. New York: Harper & Bros.

Hutchins, Robert M. (1972). The great anti-school campaign. In *The great ideas today 1972* (pp. 154–227). Chicago: Encyclopaedia Britannica.

Jackson, Philip W. (1968). *Life in classrooms*. New York: Holt, Rinehart & Winston.

Jackson, Philip W. (1992). Conceptions of curriculum and curriculum specialists. In P. W. Jackson (Ed.), *Handbook of research on curriculum* (pp. 3–40). New York: Macmillan.

Johnson, Jean, & Immerwahr, John. (1994). *First things first: What Americans expect from the public schools*. New York: Public Agenda Foundation.

Kaestle, Carl F. (Ed.). (1973). *Joseph Lancaster and the monitorial school movement: A documentary history* (Classics in Education No. 47). New York: Teachers College Press.

Kerr, Clark. (1991, February 27). Is education really all that guilty? *Education Week*, p. 30.

Kerr, Donna H. (1987). Authority and responsibility in public schooling. In J. I. Goodlad (Ed.), *The ecology of school renewal* (pp. 20–40), Eighty-sixth yearbook of the National Society for the Study of Education, Pt. I. Chicago: University of Chicago Press.

Kerr, Donna H. (1993). *Beyond education: In search of nurture*, Work in Progress Series, No. 2. Seattle, WA: Institute for Educational Inquiry.

Kerr, Donna H. (1996). Democracy, nurturance, and community. In R. Soder (Ed.), *Democracy, education, and the schools* (pp. 37–68). San Francisco: Jossey-Bass.

Kerr, Donna H. (in press). Toward a democratic rhetoric of schooling. In J. I. Goodlad & T. J. McMannon (Eds.), *The public purpose of education and schooling*. San Francisco: Jossey-Bass.

Kidder, Tracy. (1989). *Among schoolchildren*. Boston: Houghton Mifflin.

Klein, M. Frances. (1980). *Teacher perceived sources of influence on what is taught in subject areas* (Tech. Rep. No. 15, A Study of Schooling in the United States). Los Angeles: University of California, Graduate School of Education, Laboratory in School and Community Education.

La Belle, Thomas J. (1975). Alternative educational strategies: The integration of learning systems in the community. In J. I. Goodlad et al., *The conventional and the alternative in education* (pp. 165–187). Berkeley, CA: McCutchan.

Ladd, Everett C. (1996, June/July). The data just don't show erosion of America's "social capital." *The Public Perspective*, 7 (1), 5–6.

Lawson, Hal A. (1995, January). Schools and educational communities in a new vision for child welfare. *Journal for a Just and Caring Education*, *1*, 5–26.

Lawson, Hal A. (1996, Spring). Expanding the Goodlad agenda: Interprofessional education and community collaboration in service of vulnerable children, youth, and families. *Holistic Education Review*, *9*, 20–34.

Lightfoot, Sara Lawrence. (1983). *The good high school*. New York: Basic Books.

Lightman, Alan. (1993). *Einstein's dreams*. New York: Pantheon.

Loh, Wallace D. (1994, July 3). America: A nation of nations. *Seattle Post-Intelligencer*, p. E3.

Lynd, Albert. (1953). *Quackery in the public schools*. Boston: Little, Brown.

Machlup, Fritz. (1970). *Education and economic growth*. Lincoln: University of Nebraska Press.

Malen, Betty. (1994). The micropolitics of education: Mapping the multiple dimensions of power relations in school politics. In *Politics of Education Association Yearbook 1994* (pp. 147–167). New York: Falmer Press.

Marshall, Ray, & Tucker, Marc. (1992). *Thinking for a living: Education and the wealth of nations*. New York: Basic Books.

Martin, Jane Roland. (1992). *The schoolhome*. Cambridge, MA: Harvard University Press.

Mathews, David. (1996). *Is there a public for public schools?* Dayton, OH: Kettering Foundation Press.

McCraw, Thomas K. (1994, Winter). The strategic vision of Alexander Hamilton. *The American Scholar, 63*, 31–57.

McMannon, Timothy J. (1995). *Morality, efficiency, and reform: An interpretation of the history of American education*, Work in Progress Series, No. 5. Seattle, WA: Institute for Educational Inquiry.

McNeil, Linda M. (1986). *Contradictions of control: School structure and school knowledge*. New York: Routledge, Chapman, & Hall.

Miller, L. Scott. (1995). *An American imperative: Accelerating minority educational advancement*. New Haven, CT: Yale University Press.

Miller, Ron. (1990, Spring). Editorial: Education in a declining culture. *Holistic Education Review, 3*, 2–3.

Molinaro, Matie, McLuhan, Corinne, & Toye, William. (1987). *Letters of Marshall McLuhan*. New York: Oxford University Press.

Morefield, John W. *Recreating schools for all children* (Position paper). Seattle, WA: Hawthorne Elementary School.

Myrdal, Gunnar. (1944). *An American dilemma: The negro problem and modern democracy*, 2 vols. New York: Harper.

National Board for Professional Teaching Standards. (1989). *Toward high and rigorous standards for the teaching profession*. Detroit, MI: Author.

National Commission on Excellence in Education. (1983). *A nation at risk*. Washington, DC: Government Printing Office.

National Governors' Association. (1986). *Time for results*. Washington, DC: Author.

Noddings, Nel. (1984). *Caring: A feminine approach to ethics and moral education*. Berkeley: University of California Press.

Noddings, Nel. (1992). *The challenge to care in schools: An alternative approach to education*. New York: Teachers College Press.

Oakes, Jeannie. (1985). *Keeping track: How schools structure inequality*. New Haven, CT: Yale University Press.

Oakeshott, Michael. (1991). *Rationalism in politics and other essays* (Expanded ed.). Indianapolis, IN: Liberty Press.

Osguthorpe, Russell T., Harris, R. Carl, Harris, Melanie Fox, & Black, Sharon (Eds.). (1995). *Partner schools: Centers for educational renewal*. San Francisco: Jossey-Bass.

Parker, Walter C. (Ed.). (1996). *Educating the democratic mind*. Albany: State University of New York Press.

Peter, Laurence Johnston. (1969). *The Peter principle*. New York: Morrow.

Peters, Thomas J., & Waterman, Robert H. (1982). *In search of excellence*. New York: Harper & Row.

Phenix, Philip H. (1961). Education and the concept of man. In *Views and ideas on mankind*, Bulletin No. 9. Chicago: Committee on the Study of Mankind.

Plecki, Margaret L. (1991). *The relationship of elementary school size and student achievement in California public schools*. Unpublished doctoral dissertation, University of California, Berkeley.

Plecki, Margaret L. (1992, April). *The relationship between middle school size and student achievement*. Paper presented at the annual meeting of the American Educational Research Association, San Francisco.

Pomfret, John D. (1996, February 17). Letter to the editor. *Seattle Post-Intelligencer*, p. A7.

Pusey, Nathan M. (1963). *The age of the scholar*. Cambridge, MA: Belknap Press of Harvard University Press.

Putnam, Robert D. (1993). *Making democracy work: Civic traditions in modern Italy*. Princeton, NJ: Princeton University Press.

Putnam, Robert D. (1995, January). Bowling alone: America's declining social capital. *Journal of Democracy, 6*, 65–78.

Quinn, Daniel. (1992). *Ishmael*. New York: Bantam/Turner.

Richman, Sheldon. (1994). *Separating school and state: How to liberate America's families*. Fairfax, VA: The Future of Freedom Foundation.

Riley, Michael N. (1992, November). If it looks like manure . . . *Phi Delta Kappan, 74*, 239–241.

Rosen, Robert. (1974, February). Do we really need ends to justify the means? *Center Report*. Santa Barbara, CA: Center for the Study of Democratic Institutions.

Ryan, Alan. (1995). *John Dewey and the high tide of American liberalism*. New York: W. W. Norton.

Sacks, Oliver. (1987). *The man who mistook his wife for a hat*. New York: Harper & Row, Perennial Library Edition.

Sandel, Michael J. (1984). The procedural republic and the unencumbered self. *Political Theory, 12*, 81–96.

Sarason, Seymour B. (1972). *The creation of settings and the future societies*. San Francisco: Jossey-Bass.

Sarason, Seymour B. (1996). *Revisiting "The culture of the school and the problem of change"* (3rd ed.). New York: Teachers College Press.

Sarason, Seymour B. (1986, August). And what is the public interest? *American Psychologist, 41*, 899–905.

Sarason, Seymour B. (1990). *The predictable failure of educational reform: Can we change course before it's too late?* San Francisco: Jossey-Bass.

Sarason, Seymour B. (1993). American psychology, and the needs for transcendence and community. *American Journal of Community Psychology, 21* (2), 185–202.

Scheffler, Israel. (1976). Basic mathematical skills: Some philosophical and practical remarks. *Teachers College Record, 78*, 205–212.

Schultz, Theodore W. (1971). *Investment in human capital: The role of education and of research.* New York: Free Press.

Simpson, Stephen. (1974). *The working man's manual.* Cited in S. Cohen (Ed.), The Working Man's Party of Philadelphia calls for free, equal education for all (1831), in *Education in the United States: A documentary history* (pp. 1054–1056). New York: Random House.

Sirotnik, Kenneth A. (1989). The school as the center of change. In T. J. Sergiovanni & J. H. Moore (Eds.), *Schooling for tomorrow: Directing reform to issues that count.* Newton, MA: Allyn & Bacon.

Sirotnik, Kenneth A. (in press). Ecological images of change: Limits and possibilities. In A. Hargreaves, A. Lieberman, M. Fullan, & D. Hopkins (Eds.) & A. Lieberman (Vol. Ed.), *International handbook on educational change: Vol. 1. Roots of educational change.* Dordrecht, The Netherlands: Kluwer Press.

Sirotnik, Kenneth A., & Goodlad, John I. (1988). *School-university partnerships: Concepts, cases, and concerns.* New York: Teachers College Press.

Sizer, Theodore R. (1984). *High school reform and the reform of teacher education.* Ninth annual DeGarmo Lecture, University of Minnesota, Minneapolis.

Sizer, Theodore R. (1984). *Horace's school.* Boston: Houghton Mifflin.

Sizer, Theodore R. (in press). The meanings of "public education." In J. I. Goodlad & T. J. McMannon (Eds.), *The public purpose of education and schooling.* San Francisco: Jossey-Bass.

Skinner, B. F. (1962). *Walden two.* New York: Macmillan.

Smith, Mary Lee, & Noble, Audrey J. (1993). Toward a comprehensive program of evaluation. In J. I. Goodlad & T. C. Lovitt (Eds.), *Integrating general and special education* (pp. 149–170). New York: Macmillan.

Smith, Mortimer B. (1949). *And madly teach.* Chicago: Henry Regnery.

Stapledon, Olaf. (1968). *Last and first men.* New York: Dover Publications. (Original work published 1931)

Strauss, Leo. (1952). *The political philosophy of Hobbes: Its basis and its genesis* (E. M. Sinclair, Trans.). Chicago: University of Chicago Press.

Tarcov, Nathan. (1996). The meanings of democracy. In R. Soder (Ed.), *Democracy, education, and the schools* (pp. 1–36). San Francisco: Jossey-Bass.

Task Force on Early Childhood Education. (1972). *Early childhood education.* Sacramento: California State Department of Education.

Teilhard de Chardin, Pierre. (1961). *The phenomenon of man.* New York: Harper & Row.

Tocqueville, Alexis de. (1969). *Democracy in America* (G. Lawrence, Trans.). New York: Anchor Books.

Tyack, David B., & Hansot, Elisabeth. (1982). *Managers of virtue: Public school leadership in America, 1820–1980*. New York: Basic Books.

Tyler, Ralph W. (1994). Why do we have public schools in a democracy? Foreword to J. I. Goodlad, *What schools are for* (2nd ed., pp. vii–viii). Bloomington, IN: Phi Delta Kappa Educational Foundation.

Ulich, Robert. (1955). *The human career: A philosophy of self-transcendence*. New York: Harper & Row.

Ulich, Robert. (1964). The ambiguities in the great movements of thought. In R. Ulich (Ed.), *Education and the idea of mankind* (pp. 3–33). New York: Harcourt, Brace, & World.

Underwood, Julie K. (1995, Spring). School finance adequacy as vertical equity. *University of Michigan Journal of Law Reform, 29*, 495–496.

Vandenberg, Donald. (1990). *Education as a human right: A theory of curriculum and pedagogy*. New York: Teachers College Press.

van der Post, Laurens. (1974). *A far-off place*. San Diego: Harcourt Brace.

Viviano, Frank. (1993, September/October). The fall of Rome. *Mother Jones, 18*, 37–40.

Wagar, Warren W. (1967). *The city of man: Prophecies of a world civilization in twentieth-century thought* (Rpt. ed.). Boston: Houghton Mifflin. (Original work published 1963)

Wagar, Warren W. (1971). Religion, ideology, and the idea of mankind in contemporary history. In W. W. Wagar (Ed.), *History and the idea of mankind* (pp. 196–221). Albuquerque: University of New Mexico.

Wehlage, Gary, Smith, Gregory, & Lipman, Pauline. (1992, Spring). Restructuring urban schools: The new futures experience. *American Educational Research Journal, 29* (Spring), 51–93.

Westbrook, Robert B. (1991). *John Dewey and American democracy*. Ithaca, NY: Cornell University Press.

Westbrook, Robert B. (1996). Public schooling and American democracy. In R. Soder (Ed.), *Democracy, education, and the schools* (pp. 125–150). San Francisco: Jossey-Bass.

White, John. (1991). *Education and the good life*. New York: Teachers College Press.

William T. Grant Foundation Commission on Work, Family and Community. (1988). *The forgotten half: Pathways to success for America's youth and young families*. Washington, DC: The Commission.

Wirth, Arthur G. (1981). What we can learn from our experiences with the Deweyan tradition. In L. N. Tanner (Ed.), *Papers of the society for the study of curriculum history* (pp. 3–5). (ERIC Document Reproduction Service No. ED 216 995)

Index

About the Author

John I. Goodlad is co-director of the Center for Educational Renewal, University of Washington, and president of the Institute for Educational Inquiry. In addition to advancing a comprehensive program of research and development directed to the simultaneous renewal of schooling and teacher education, he is inquiring into the mission of education in a democratic society to which such renewal must be directed.